HANDBOOK FOR TODAY'S CATHOLIC

Fully indexed to the
Catechism of the Catholic Church

FOREWORD BY
JOHN CARDINAL O'CONNOR

A REDEMPTORIST
PASTORAL PUBLICATION

Liguori
ONE LIGUORI DRIVE
LIGUORI MO 63057-9999

Imprimi Potest:
James Shea, C.SS.R.
Provincial, St. Louis Province
The Redemptorists

Imprimatur:
+ Edward J.O'Donnell, D.D.
Archdiocesan Administrator, Archdiocese of St. Louis

ISBN 0-89243-671-9
Library of Congress Catalog Card Number: 94-75247

To order, call 1-800-325-9521
www.liguori.org
www.catholicbooksonline.com

Cover design by Myra Roth

CONTENTS

SECTION TWO: PRACTICES

SECTION THREE: PRAYERS

FOREWORD

The story of John the Baptizer is beautifully told in the first chapter of the Gospel of Saint John.

> A man named John was sent from God. He came for testimony, to testify to the light, so that all might believe through him. He was not the light, but came to testify to the light. The true light, which enlightens everyone, was coming into the world (1:6-9).

Every person who is baptized into the Catholic Church bears the same awesome responsibility of the Baptizer himself: to be a witness to the Light. For indeed the Light has come into the world: Christ, the Son of God!

Our task as witnesses to Christ is complicated in an age filled with temptations toward self-aggrandizement and material desires. Much of the advertising and entertainment in our culture attempts to persuade us that our earthly life is all there is, so we should pursue the pleasures and successes of this world. The concept of heaven is ridiculed, and the idea of sin is dismissed as archaic.

The Catholic knows that he or she is *not* the Light, and that life on this earth is only a pilgrimage toward the life with God promised to those who believe, to those who are faithful witnesses to the Light. We need not despair in our efforts, for we have been given at least three important means of following the call of Isaiah that John the Baptizer made his own, "Make straight the way of the Lord" (1:23).

The first is constant prayer. Whether it be the prayer of the Church called the Divine Office, the rosary, the beautiful prayers to our Blessed Mother, or the simple prayers of meditation when we seek to do what our Lord himself asked, "Be still and [know] that I am God" (Psalm 46:11), our conversations with God draw us to the Light, revealing him to each of us very personally. Prayer reawakens in us the recognition that Christ alone is the Light to the world.

The second gift we are given is grace, which comes to us through the sacraments of the Church. Frequent participation in the sacraments, especially the sacraments of penance and Eucharist, brings us the grace of the Light. It is this grace that strengthens us in our resolve to be faithful witnesses to Christ.

Finally, we are given the teachings of the Church. Timeless in their applicability, these teachings proclaim the primacy of the Light, who is the Alpha and the Omega. Those who are his witnesses are made in his image and likeness.

I am pleased to introduce the *Handbook for Today's Catholic.* It is an easy-to-use guide to prayer, the sacraments, and the teachings of the Church. Indexed to the new *Catechism of the Catholic Church,* the *Handbook* is an important and very usable companion for every Catholic. It is my hope that those who read the *Handbook* may be inspired to delve into the *Catechism* itself. Both will enable Catholics to meet the challenge to take their faith seriously, to comprehend it intelligently, and to demonstrate it passionately in their daily lives.

May this *Handbook* be used to help us fulfill our task, with John the Baptizer, to go forth as witnesses to testify to the Light.

JOHN CARDINAL O'CONNOR (1920-2000)
ARCHBISHOP OF NEW YORK

PREFACE

This book first appeared in 1978. In 1991, it was revised and expanded, and to date, more than four million copies have found their way into the homes of the faithful. This edition of the *Handbook* appears once again not only as a presentation of the most basic Catholic beliefs, practices, and prayers but also as an edition that is fully indexed to the new *Catechism of the Catholic Church: Libreria Editrice Vaticana.* The *Catechism* is the official documentation of the truths that Catholics believe. This booklet is not a condensation of the *Catechism* but rather a reference edition of the *Handbook,* designed for your information and convenience.

The men and women of the pastoral team of Liguori Publications take this opportunity to express their heartfelt gratitude to John Cardinal O'Connor, Archbishop of New York, for his willingness to contribute the Foreword to this edition. Through the intercession of St. Alphonsus Liguori, may all those who read this booklet be filled with wisdom, understanding, and love.

ROBERT PAGLIARI, C.SS.R.
EDITOR-IN-CHIEF
PRINT AND ELECTRONIC MEDIA DEPARTMENT

INTRODUCTION

BY CHARLENE ALTEMOSE, MSC

Our lifestyles, as well as our "faith-styles," have changed dramatically in the last generation. Scientific advances and streamlined communication methods have revolutionized not only our daily lives but also our understanding of the spiritual life. How we think and live influence the ways we relate to God and religion.

In 1962 Pope John XXIII, realizing that the Church needed to develop more meaningful ways of ministering in the modern age, called together the bishops of the world for the Second Vatican Council, or Vatican II. The renewal brought about by this historic assembly radically changed how Catholics understand and practice the Faith today.

To be truly Catholic is to live according to the spirit and attitude launched by the Second Vatican Council. However, because the Catholic Church traces its origins back to Christ and the early Christian community, it treasures its centuries of Tradition as well. To integrate the revered teachings of the past with the changes of modern times is the challenge Catholics face today. Whether you are Catholic by heritage or by a faith decision made later in life, you are called to live your baptismal commitment in every aspect of your life. The contemporary Catholic, in the midst of the complexities of modern life, shares an ancient historical legacy with a community of believers, accepts the insights of Vatican II, and forges ahead toward the future with hope.

The basic purpose of this *Handbook* is to provide information on the essentials of Catholicism and to enlighten all who wish to live out the teachings of Vatican II. Toward those ends, this edition of the *Handbook* has been fully indexed to the *Catechism of the Catholic Church*. Throughout the text, the numerical citations direct you to the segment of the *Catechism* where specific topics and subjects are explained.

Section One: Beliefs. What Catholics believe about God, the Trinity, Jesus, the Church, the sacraments, and other dogmas comprise the "sacred deposit of the Word of God." These truths express in human terms our understanding of who God is and what has been revealed through Jesus and the Church.

The Nicene Creed, which Catholics recite at the Sunday liturgy, summarizes our basic beliefs about God. In this section we discuss major Catholic doctrines not only as objective facts but as spiritual realities that are intimately connected to a lived-out faith life. They are "truths Catholics live by."

Section Two: Practices. The Ten Commandments are the moral norms for Catholics. Over the years the Church has developed the Precepts of the Church, time-honored observances to guide Catholics in living according to Church teaching. Section Two also contains practical points about the sacraments, the holy days, and other Catholic traditions.

Section Three: Prayers. Catholics firmly believe that a living faith includes communicating with God on a personal level. In Section Three we consider the basic prayer forms that are part of Catholic tradition. Catholics are encouraged to meditate on Scripture and inspirational writings for a well-rounded spiritual life.

Section Four: Living the Faith in the Spirit of Vatican II. In this expanded edition of the *Handbook*, Section Four has been added to provide an overview of insights and changes brought about by Vatican II. It discusses practical applications of post-Vatican II Catholicism regarding Scripture, liturgy and sacraments, ministries in the Church, life commitments, social responsibility, evangelization and the RCIA, and attitudes toward other religions.

"A Guide to Action for Today's Catholic" draws together important aspects of what it means to "Live in the Spirit of Vatican II."

Since Vatican II provides guidelines for renewal, we include an outline of the sixteen Documents of Vatican II, which Pope Paul VI called "the great catechism of our times."

SECTION ONE
BELIEFS

1. You the Seeker, God the Seeker

You: A Human Being Who Seeks God
[1, 1701-1715]

From the time you learned to talk, you asked questions—which reveals something absolutely basic about you: the fact that you have a questioning *intellect.*

Throughout your life, you have always wanted things, and you find yourself making constant decisions—saying yes to this, no to that. These experiences reveal something else very basic about you: the fact that you have a free *will*, the power to want and to choose [1-3].

As time passes you are changing in bodily appearance, and your way of viewing life is shifting and deepening. But the basic you—the "I" behind your eyes—remains the same person. At your core you are constantly reaching out, seeking that for which you were created. This questing, spiritual core of your being has been called by many names. Common names for it are *soul*, *spirit*, or *heart* [27, 44-47].

The Ultimate Reality you seek—which is present in everything you reach out to—has also been called by many names. The most common name for this Ultimate Reality is *God* [43]. You are so bound to God that without him you would not live or move or have your being. You are so bound to God that if you did not sense his presence in some way, you would view life as pointless and cease to seek... [1701-1715, 1718].

God: The Divine Lover Who Found You
[50-53, 142, 1719]

Meanwhile, as you seek God, God seeks you. The Vatican II *Dogmatic Constitution on Divine Revelation* expresses it this way: "The invisible God, from the fullness of his love, addresses men as his friends, and moves among them, in order to invite and receive them into his own company" (2) [1719].

As a Catholic you are called to seek and find Christ. But you did not begin this quest on your own initiative. The initiative was all God's. All who follow Christ were once lost but were searched for and found. God first found you and made you visibly his in baptism. What he seeks now is that you seek him. In a mysterious way your whole life with God is an ongoing quest for each other by two lovers—God and you—who already possess each other [50-53, 521].

2. Revelation, Faith, Doctrine, and Doubt
Revelation and Faith
[50-64]

God seeks you—which is why he has chosen to "manifest and communicate both himself and the eternal decrees of his will concerning the salvation of mankind" (*Revelation*, 6). In revealing, God has not only communicated information; he has communicated *himself* to you [36-38, 51-53].

Your personal response to God's communication of himself and his will is called *faith*. "By faith man freely commits his entire self to God, making 'the full submission of his intellect and will to God who reveals,' and willingly assenting to the Revelation given by him" (*Revelation*, 5) [142, 143, 153-164, 1814-1816].

Catholic Doctrine
[84-100]

The basic doctrines, or dogmas, of the Church are the verbal expression of what God has revealed to us about our relationship with him. The key characteristic of the Church's dogmas is that they agree with sacred

Scripture. The teachings spell out the unchangeable content of revelation, translating it into the changeable thought-forms and languages of people in every new era and culture. A dogma is a statement of truth, a formulation of some aspect of the Faith. The purpose of each dogma is to bring Jesus Christ to our attention from a particular point of view. As a coherent set of teachings, Church dogma is a faithful interpretation of God's self-communication to humankind [88-100, 170-171].

Faith and Doubt

The Church's dogmatic formulas, however, are not the same thing as God's self-revelation; they are the *medium* through which Catholics place their faith in God. God unveils and communicates the hidden mystery of himself *through* Church teachings. The teachings are like sacraments through which you receive God. Through the medium of doctrinal formulas, you reach God himself in the personal act of faith [88-90].

The life of faith is very personal and delicate—and ultimately mysterious. Faith is a gift of God and only God knows who has it. We can, however, presume that God is generous with his gift, and we should not presume that anyone lacks it [153].

A person can lack faith through his or her own fault; we are free— even to reject God. But when a person "doubts," we should not jump to conclusions. For example, there are people who remember their father as a man who inflicted pain on them. As a result these people cannot bring themselves to believe in God as their "good Father." This is not a lack of faith. It is a lack of memory images through which these persons can appreciate God as Father. Negative mental images can block a person from receiving God's self-revelation in a particular form. But such images cannot block out all forms in which people perceive and express God's mystery. God, who seeks us constantly, seeks us until we find him [215].

A person who is seeking deeper insight into reality may sometimes have doubts, even about God himself. Such doubts do not necessarily indicate a lack of faith. They may be just the opposite—a sign of growing faith. Faith is alive and dynamic. It seeks, through grace, to penetrate into

15

the very mystery of God. If a particular doctrine of faith no longer makes sense to a person, the person should go right on seeking. To know what a doctrine says is one thing; to gain an insight into its meaning through the gift of understanding is something else. When in doubt, "Seek and you will find." The person who seeks by reading, discussing, thinking, or praying eventually sees light. The person who talks to God even when God is "not there" is alive with faith [162].

3. One God, Three Divine Persons
[232-267]

The Catholic Church teaches that the fathomless mystery we call God has revealed himself to humankind as a Trinity of Persons—the Father, the Son, and the Holy Spirit [238-248].

Three Persons, One God
[249-267]

The mystery of the Trinity is the central doctrine of Catholic faith. Upon it are based all other teachings of the Church. In the New Testament there is frequent mention of the Father, the Son, and the Holy Spirit. A careful reading of these passages leads to one unmistakable conclusion: each Person is presented as having qualities that can belong only to God. But if there is only one God, how can this be [199-202]?

The Church studied this mystery with great care and, after four centuries of clarification, decided to state the doctrine in this way: in the unity of the Godhead there are three Persons—the Father, the Son, and the Holy Spirit—truly distinct one from another. Thus, in the words of the Athanasian Creed: "The Father is God, the Son is God, and the Holy Spirit is God, and yet there are not three gods but one God" [249-256].

Creator, Savior, Sanctifier
[257-260]

All effects of God's action upon his creatures are produced by the three divine Persons in common. But because certain effects of the divine action in creation remind us more of one divine Person than another, the Church ascribes particular effects to one or the other divine Person. Thus, we speak of the Father as Creator of all that is, of the Son, the Word of God, as our Savior or Redeemer, and of the Holy Spirit—the love of God "poured into our hearts"—as our Sanctifier [234-237].

To believe that God is Father means to believe that you are son or daughter; that God your Father accepts and loves you; that God your Father has created you as a love-worthy human being [238-240].

To believe that God is saving Word means to believe that you are a listener; that your response to God's Word is to open yourself to his liberating gospel which frees you to choose union with God and brotherhood with your neighbor [2716, 2724].

To believe that God is Spirit means to believe that on this earth you are meant to live a sanctifying, supernatural life that is a created sharing in God's own nature—a life which is the beginning of life eternal [1691, 1703, 1704].

4. God, the Father of Jesus
[198-267]

The Book of Exodus records one of the most profound revelations in human history. The revelation is narrated in the story of God calling Moses to be the leader of his people. Speaking from a burning bush, which "though on fire, was not consumed," God called out: "Moses! Moses!" God then told Moses to organize the Israelites and persuade Pharaoh to let him lead that enslaved people out of Egypt. Hearing the plan, Moses was apprehensive. The dialogue goes [204, 210, 211]:

> "But," said Moses to God, "when I go to the Israelites and say to them, 'The God of your fathers has sent me to you,' if they ask me, 'What is his name?' what am I to tell them?" God replied, "I am who am." Then he added, "This is what you shall tell the Israelites: I AM sent me to you" [446, 2575].

> God spoke further to Moses, "Thus shall you say to the Israelites: The LORD, the God of your fathers, the God of Abraham, the God of Isaac, the God of Jacob, has sent me to you."
>
> Exodus 3:13-15

In this dialogue (and in others like it—read Judges 13:18 and Genesis 32:30), God does not really give himself a "name." He refuses to give himself a "handle" that could leave people the impression they "have a handle" on God. God says, in effect, that he is not like any of the many gods people worship. He conceals himself—thereby revealing the infinite distance between himself and all that we human beings try to know and control [205-208].

But by telling Moses to say, "I AM sent me to you," God also reveals something very personal. This God who "is," beyond all realities that come and go, is not unconnected with us and our world. On the contrary, this God who "is" reveals that he is *with you*. He does not tell *what* he is *in himself*. But he does reveal *who* he is *to you*. In this key moment recorded in Exodus (and developed further in the Book of Isaiah, chapters 40-45), God revealed that he is *your* God, the "God of your fathers"—the fathomless mystery who is with you through all time, with you beyond all powers of death and evil [214-221, 2810].

The God who reveals himself in the Old Testament has two main characteristics. First, and most important, is the revelation that he is personally close to you, that he is *your* God. Second is the fact that this God who freely chooses a personal relationship with you is beyond all time and space. I AM is bound to nothing, but binds all things to himself. In his own words, "I am the first and I am the last; / there is no God but me" (Isaiah 44:6) [198, 212].

Centuries after the revelation reflected in Exodus and Isaiah, the mysterious God of the burning bush did reveal his name—in Person. Shattering all human assumptions and expectations, God's Word "became flesh and made his dwelling among us" (John 1:14) [65, 73]. In a revelation that blinds the mind with its light, Jesus spoke to I AM and said: "Father, [you] are in me and I in you…I made known to them your name and I will make it known, that the love with which you loved me may be in them and I in them" (John 17:21, 26) [260, 422-425, 820, 2750].

I AM reveals his name in his Son. The burning bush draws you into its light. The God of Moses, revealed in Jesus, is love, is Father, is in you [211, 218-221, 587-591].

5. Jesus Christ

[422-682]

Jesus, God and Man

[464-469]

The second Person of the Blessed Trinity became a man, Jesus Christ. His mother was Mary of Nazareth, daughter of Joachim and Anne. Joseph, Mary's husband, was like a father to Jesus. Jesus' true and only Father is God; he had no human father [525, 526].

Conceived in Mary's womb by the power of the Holy Spirit, Jesus was born in Bethlehem of Judea, probably between the years 6 and 4 B.C. [484, 487]. He died on Calvary (outside of Old Jerusalem) as a relatively young man, most likely in his early thirties [595-623].

He is only one Person, but he has both a divine nature and a human nature. He is truly God, and he is also truly a human being. As God, he has all the qualities and attributes of God. As human, he has a human body, human soul, human mind and will, human imagination, and human feelings. His divinity does not overwhelm or interfere with his humanity—and vice versa [464-478].

On Calvary he really died; he experienced the same kind of death that all human beings experience. But during his dying, at his death, and after his death, he remained God [595-623].

After his death, Jesus "descended to the dead." The older English translation of the Creed said "descended into hell"—which means the same thing: *Hades*, the nether world, the region of the dead, the condition of those who had passed on from this life. (This is clear from New Testament references such as 1 Peter 3:19ff, 4:6; Ephesians 4:9; Romans 10:7; Matthew 12:40; Acts 2:27, 31.) Basically, therefore, "descended to the dead" means Jesus really died and entered among the dead as their Savior. Liturgically, Holy Saturday expresses this aspect of the mystery of salvation—the "death" or absence of God [631-637].

The prayer of the dying Jesus—"My God, my God, why have you forsaken me?" (Mark 15:34)—finds its echo in the lives of many Christians. "Descended to the dead" expresses Jesus' outcry of agony his experience of clinging to his Father in his moment of absolute anguish. It also expresses what many Catholics experience as God deepens their love of him by making them realize the hell life is without a sense of his presence [618].

Jesus rose from the dead on Easter morning. He is living today with his Father and the Spirit—and in our midst. He is still both God and man and always will be [638-658].

He lives. And his passage from death to life is the mystery of salvation we are all meant to share [655, 658].

Christ, the Revelation and Sacrament of God
[65-67]

By his preaching, and by his death and resurrection, Jesus is both the revealer and the *revelation of God*. Who the Father is, is shown in his Son, Jesus. As the revelation of God, Jesus is both God's approach to human-kind and our path to God [73, 422-425].

Jesus is the ultimate sign of God's salvation in the world—the center and means of God's encounter with you. Thus, we call him the *original sacrament*. The grace he communicates to you is himself. Through this communication of himself, you receive the total self-communication of God. Jesus is the saving presence of God in the world [519,520,1113-1116].

Christ, the Center of Your Life
[426-429]

Jesus comes to you, actively influencing your life in various ways. He comes to you in his Word—when the Word of God is preached to you or when you read the Scriptures with attentive reverence [101-104]. He is also present to you in the seven sacraments—especially in the Eucharist [1373]. Another way you meet Jesus is in other people. As we read in the Final Judgment scene in the Gospel of Matthew, "Then the righteous will answer him and say, 'Lord, when did we see you hungry and feed you, or thirsty and give you drink?'...And the king will say to them in reply, 'Amen, I say to you, whatever you did for one of these least brothers of mine, you did for me'" (25:37, 40) [678, 1503, 1939, 2449].

The Catholic Church believes that Jesus of Nazareth is the center of our lives and destiny. In the document *Pastoral Constitution on the Church in the Modern World*, Vatican II affirms that Jesus is "the key, the center and the purpose of the whole of man's history" (10). With Saint Paul, the Church believes that "many are the promises of God, their Yes is in him" (2 Corinthians 1:20) [65-73, 426-429].

6. The Holy Spirit
[683-747]

The Indwelling Spirit

There is a common way in which God is present to all of creation. Saint Paul referred to this all-enveloping presence of God when he quoted a Greek poet who said, "In him we live and move and have our being" (Acts 17:28) [28, 300].

But there is another entirely personal presence of God within those who love him. Jesus himself speaks of it in the Gospel of John, where he says: "Whoever loves me will keep my word, and my Father will love him, and we will come to him and make our dwelling with him" (14:23) [260].

This special presence of the Trinity is properly ascribed to the Holy Spirit, for as Saint Paul proclaims, "The love of God has been poured out into our hearts through the holy Spirit that has been given to us" (Romans 5:5). This presence of the Spirit, God's gift of love within you, is called the *divine indwelling* [733].

Gifts of the Spirit
[1830-1832]

The Spirit is not only intimately present within you; he is silently but actively working to transform you. If you attune yourself to his silent promptings, then the gifts of the Holy Spirit become experienced realities in your life.

There are two kinds of gifts of the Spirit. The gifts of the first kind are intended for the sanctification of the person who receives them. They are permanent supernatural qualities that enable the graced person to be especially in tune with the inspirations of the Holy Spirit. They are wisdom (which helps a person value the things of heaven), understanding (which enables the person to grasp the truths of religion), counsel (which helps one see and correctly choose the best practical approach in serving God), fortitude (which steels a person's resolve in overcoming obstacles to living the faith), knowledge (which helps one see the path to follow and the dangers to one's faith), piety (which fills a person with confidence in God and an eagerness to serve him), and fear of the Lord (which makes a person keenly aware of God's sovereignty and the respect due to him and his laws) [1830, 1831, 1845].

A second kind of gifts of the Spirit are called charisms. They are extraordinary favors granted principally for the help of others. In 1 Corinthians 12:6-11, nine charisms are mentioned. They are the gifts of speaking with wisdom, speaking with knowledge, faith, healing, miracles, prophecy, discerning of spirits, tongues, and interpreting speeches [688, 799-801, 809].

Other passages of Saint Paul (such as 1 Corinthians 12:28-31 and Romans 12:6-8) mention other charisms [736, 1508, 2004].

7. Grace and the Theological Virtues
[1996-2005, 1812-1829]

Grace: God's Life Within You
[1996-2005]

You are probably familiar with the distinction made between habitual grace (the state of sanctifying grace) and actual grace (divine help given for the performing of acts). These are two aspects of the life you live when you possess grace itself: the Spirit of God who is "poured out into our hearts" (Romans 5:5) [368, 733].

Grace is the presence to you of God's living, dynamic Spirit. As a result of this presence, you live with a new, abundant inner life that makes you "share in the divine nature" (2 Peter 1:4), a son or daughter of God, and a brother or sister—a fellow heir—with Jesus, "the firstborn among many brothers" [357]. (Read Paul's Letter to the Romans, chapter 8.)

As a result of the Spirit's presence, you live and respond to God in a totally new way. You live a "graced" life that is good, really pleasing to God. Under the Spirit's influence you live a life of love that builds up Christ's Body, the Church. Being "in the Spirit" with the rest of the Church, you live with others in such a way as to build a spirit of love and community wherever you are [1721, 1810].

Grace—God's life within you—transforms the whole meaning and direction of your life [1722, 1810]. In grace, Saint Paul declared: "For to me life is Christ, and death is gain" (Philippians 1:21) [1010, 1698]. Ultimately, grace—God's free gift of himself to you—is life eternal, a life that has already begun. Already, while you are still an earthly pilgrim, grace is "Christ in you, the hope for glory" (Colossians 1:27) [772].

Faith, Hope, and Charity
[1812-1829]

As a human being, you are capable of believing, trusting, and loving others. Grace transforms these ways you relate to others into the theological (God-directed) virtues of faith, hope, and charity—capacities to relate to God and others as one of his dearly loved sons and daughters [1810].

In the state of grace, you have *faith*: you believe in God, committing your total being to him as the personal source of all truth and reality and your own being. You have *hope*: you rest your whole meaning and future on God, whose promise to you of life everlasting with him is being fulfilled in a hidden manner even now through your graced existence. And you have *charity*: you love God as the personal *All* of your life and all persons as sharers in the destiny God desires for all—everlasting communion with himself [2086-2094].

(If people alienate themselves from God by serious sin, they lose habitual grace and the virtue of charity. But this loss does not take away their faith or hope unless they sin directly and seriously against these virtues.)

Love for God, Self, Others
[2083]

In this life, your love for God is bound together with your love of others—and these loves are bound together with your love of self.

"Whoever does not love a brother whom he has seen cannot love God whom he has not seen" (1 John 4:20) [2840]. And by God's own commandment, you are to love your neighbor *as yourself* (Matthew 19:19; 22:39) [2052]. When it comes to practical, real-life terms, fulfillment of God's commandment to love begins with a proper self-love. In order to love God as he wills, you need to respect, esteem, and reverence yourself [2055].

You increase your love of self by allowing yourself to realize, gradually and more deeply as the years go on, that *God really loves you* with a love that has no end. You are loved and you are lovable. Whenever you try to acquire or deepen this attitude about yourself, you are cooperating with the grace of God [2196].

You also increase your love for self by trying to deepen your understanding of those around you—by listening and trusting, by loving and (what is more difficult) allowing yourself to *be* loved, by being truly forgiving and (what is most difficult) seeking true personal forgiveness, by widening your circle of compassion to embrace all living creatures and the whole of nature in its beauty [2842-2845].

There is a basic principle in the New Testament writings of Saint John that goes: "Beloved, let us love one another, because love is of God; everyone who loves is begotten by God and knows God. Whoever is without love does not know God, for God is love" (1 John 4:7-8). You learn what love is by loving. By loving, you come to know God [1, 214, 221, 773, 1828].

8. The Catholic Church
[748-870]

The Church: Founded by Jesus Christ
[763-766]

The whole life of Jesus, the Word made flesh, was the foundation of the Church [514-521].

Jesus gathered to himself followers who committed themselves completely to him. Praying beforehand, Jesus then chose his inner circle—the Twelve. To the Twelve he disclosed personal knowledge of himself, spoke of his coming passion and death, and gave in-depth instruction regarding what following his way entailed. Only the Twelve were allowed to celebrate his Last Supper with him [1340].

The Twelve were called *apostles*—that is, emissaries whose mission was to be Jesus' personal representatives. He gave these apostles the full power of authority he had from the Father. The fullness of that authority is indicated in the words of the Gospel: "Amen, I say to you, whatever you bind on earth shall be bound in heaven, and whatever you loose on earth shall be loosed in heaven" (Matthew 18:18) [2, 75-77, 126].

The climax of Jesus' preparation for the Church was the Last Supper. At this meal he took bread and wine and said: "Take and eat, this is my body: take and drink, this is my blood." With these words he actually gave *himself* to them. Receiving him in this way, the Twelve entered into a union of such total intimacy with him and with one another that nothing like it had ever before taken place. At that meal they became *one body in Jesus*. That the early Church understood the depth of this communion is shown in the earliest New Testament account of the Eucharist, the words of Saint Paul: "Because the loaf of bread is one, we, though many, are one body, for we all partake of the one loaf" (1 Corinthians 10:17) [610, 1396].

At the Supper, Jesus also spoke of the "new testament." God was establishing a new relationship with humankind, a covenant sealed with the sacrificial blood of Christ himself. This new relationship was to be governed by a new law: the commandment of love [1339].

The earliest account of the Eucharist, First Corinthians, reveals what the Last Supper meant for the future of the Church. Jesus is recorded as saying, "Do this in remembrance of me" (11:24). Jesus foresaw a long time in which his presence would not be visible to his followers. He intended that the Church repeat this Supper again and again during that time. In these memorials he would be intimately present, the risen Lord of history leading his people toward that future day when he will "make all things new" (Revelation 21:5) [1044, 1323, 1341-1344].

The Last Supper was Jesus' final step before his death in preparing the Twelve. This celebration revealed how they, and their successors through the ages, were to carry out his mission of teaching, sanctifying, and governing.

According to the gospels (Matthew 16:13-19; Luke 22:31ff; John 21:15-17), the responsibility given to the apostles was given in a special way to Saint Peter. In Matthew, Jesus's words are: "And so I say to you, you are Peter, and upon this rock I will build my church, and the gates of the netherworld shall not prevail against it" (16:18). Peter is to be the visible representative of Jesus, who is the foundation of the Church. Peter is to provide the Church with unshakable leadership against any forces that would destroy what Jesus brings to his people [552, 553, 567].

Jesus' founding of the Church was completed with the sending of the Holy Spirit. The actual birth of the Church took place on the day of Pentecost. This sending of the Spirit took place publicly, just as the crucifixion of Jesus took place in public view. Since that day, the Church has shown itself to be a divine-human reality—a combination of the Spirit working and the people striving, in their human way, to co-operate with the gift of his presence and Christ's gospel [731, 732, 767, 768].

The Church as the Body of Christ
[787-796]

The image of the Church as the Body of Christ is found in the New Testament writings of Saint Paul. In chapter 10 of 1 Corinthians, Paul says that our communion with Christ comes from "the cup of blessing," which unites us in his blood, and from "the bread that we break," which unites us to his body. Because the bread is one, all of us, though many, are one body. The eucharistic body of Christ and the Church are, together, the (Mystical) Body of Christ [805-807].

In chapter 12 of both 1 Corinthians and Romans, Paul emphasizes the mutual dependence and concern we have as *members of one another*. In the Letters to the Ephesians and Colossians, the emphasis is on *Christ as our head*. God gave Christ to the Church as its head. Through Christ, God is unfolding his plan, "the mystery hidden for ages," to unite all things and to reconcile us to himself. Because this mystery is being unfolded in the Church, Ephesians calls the Church the *mystery of Christ* [669, 770-776].

26

The Church as the Sacrament of Christ
[774-776, 780]

In our own time Pope Paul VI has expressed the same truth with these words: "The Church is a mystery. It is a reality imbued with the hidden presence of God" [751-757].

When Saint Paul and Pope Paul call the Church a *mystery*, the word has the same meaning as the word *sacrament*. It means a visible sign of God's invisible presence [774].

Just as Christ is the sacrament of God, the Church is your sacrament, your visible sign, of Christ. But the Church is not a sacrament "for members only." In its *Dogmatic Constitution on the Church,* the Second Vatican Council clearly says: "Since the Church, in Christ, is in the nature of sacrament—a sign and instrument, that is, of communion with God and of unity among all men—she here purposes, for the benefit of the faithful and of the whole world, to set forth, as clearly as possible, and in the tradition laid down by earlier Councils, her own nature and universal mission" (1) [775, 1045].

In the plan that God has for the human race, the Church is *the* sacrament, *the* primary visible instrument, through which the Spirit is bringing about the total oneness that lies in store for us all [776].

This process of salvation, however, is a divine human venture. We all have a part in it. Our cooperation with the Spirit consists of becoming a Church that sees Christ in others so that others see Christ in us [779].

The Catholic People of God
[781-786]

In speaking of the Church, the Second Vatican Council emphasizes the image of the people of God more than any other one [804].

Strictly speaking, all people are the people of God. In chapters 8 and 9 of Genesis, the Bible testifies that God has a covenant relationship with all of humankind [762]. But the people-of-God image applies in a special way to Christ's New Testament followers and sheds light on important features of the Catholic community [763-766].

One important fact about Catholics is this: we have a sense of *being*

27

a people. Even though we are made up of the most varied ethnic and national groups, we have a sense of *belonging* to the same worldwide family [815].

Another thing about the Catholic people is our sense of *history*. Our family line reaches back to earliest Christianity. Few of us know the whole panorama of our history as a Church. But most of us know stories of martyrs and saints. We know of groups, ancient and modern, who have endured persecution for the faith. And deep down we identify with these people and their history. All those generations who went before us are your people and mine [813-816, 834].

Our sense of being a people goes very deep. There may be lapsed Catholics and nonpracticing Catholics. But good or bad, they are Catholics. When they want to come back, they know where home is. And when they do come home, they are welcomed. The Church has its imperfections. But at its heart is the endless stream of God's mercy and forgiveness [827].

The Catholic community is not the whole of God's people. But it is that strong, identifiable core group who realize where we are all going [834]. Like the Old Testament people trudging toward the Promised Land, we are keenly aware that "here we have no lasting city, but we seek the one that is to come" (Hebrews 13:14). Our faith instinct tells us that God is in our future and that we need one another to reach him. This is part of our strength, a facet of our mystery [2796].

The Catholic Church: A Unique Institution
[811-870]

In the sixteenth century Cardinal Robert Bellarmine wrote: "The one and true Church is the community of men brought together by the profession of the same Christian faith and conjoined in the communion of the same sacraments, under the government of the legitimate pastors and especially the one vicar of Christ on earth, the Roman pontiff."

As a definition of the Church, the Bellarmine statement is incomplete; it speaks of the Church only as a visible institution. A more complete definition would note, as Pope Paul VI has done, that "the Church is a

28

mystery…imbued with the hidden presence of God." But the Bellarmine definition lays stress on an important point: the Church *is* a visible social reality; it has an institutional side to its make-up. From the earliest years of its history, Christianity has had a visible structure: appointed leaders, prescribed forms of worship, and approved formulas of faith. Seen in terms of these elements, the Catholic Church is a visible society. Because it is also a mystery, however, the Church is unlike any other organized group [771-779].

As a visible society, the Catholic Church is unique. Other Christian churches possess some of the same basic characteristics in common with it, such as the gifts of "one Lord, one faith, one baptism; one God and Father of all" (Ephesians 4:5-6). But as Vatican II points out, "Since these are gifts belonging to the Church of Christ, they are forces impelling towards Catholic unity" (*The Church,* 8) [771, 819, 827].

Furthermore—and this is a decisive point regarding the uniqueness of the Catholic Church—Vatican II states that "this Church, constituted and organized as a society in the present world, *subsists in the Catholic Church…*" (*The Church,* 8). This key statement teaches that the basic fullness of the Church, the vital source of complete Christian unity in the future, is found uniquely in the visible Catholic Church [816, 819, 870].

Infallibility in the Church
[889-892]

Christ gave to the Church the task of proclaiming his Good News. (See Matthew 28:19-20.) He also promised us his Spirit, who guides us "to all truth" (John 16:13). That mandate and that promise guarantee that we the Church will never fall away from Christ's teaching. This inability of the Church as a whole to stray into error regarding basic matters of Christ's teaching is called *infallibility* [2035, 2051].

The pope's responsibility is to preserve and nourish the Church. This means striving to realize Christ's Last Supper prayer to his Father, "That they may all be one, as you, Father, are in me and I in you, that they also may be in us, that the world may believe that you sent me" (John 17:21) [820].

Church teaching has a sacramental side to it; it is meant to be a sign and instrument of unity. Because the pope's responsibility is also to be a sacramental source of unity, he has a special role in regard to the Church's infallibility [820, 936, 937].

The Church's sacramental infallibility is preserved by its key instrument of infallibility, the pope. The infallibility which the whole Church has belongs to the pope in a special way. The Spirit of truth guarantees that when the pope declares that he is teaching infallibly as Christ's representative and visible head of the Church on basic matters of faith or morals, he cannot lead the Church into error. This gift from the Spirit is called papal infallibility [891].

Speaking of the infallibility of the Church, the pope, and the bishops, Vatican II says: "This infallibility, however, with which the divine redeemer wished to endow his Church in defining doctrine pertaining to faith and morals, is co-extensive with the deposit of revelation, which must be religiously guarded and loyally and courageously expounded. The Roman Pontiff, head of the college of bishops, enjoys this infallibility in virtue of his office....The infallibility promised to the Church is also present in the body of bishops when, together with Peter's successor, they exercise the supreme teaching office" (*The Church,* 25) [877, 935].

9. Mary, Mother of Jesus and of the Church

[484-511, 963-975]

In his book *Mary and Your Everyday Life,* theologian Bernard Häring remarks: "The Second Vatican Council has crowned the *Dogmatic Constitution on the Church* with a beautiful chapter on Mary, the prototype and model of the Church. The Church cannot come to a full understanding of union with Christ and service to his Gospel without a profound love and knowledge of Mary, the Mother of our Lord and ourselves." With keen insight into the deeply personal nature of salvation, Vatican II focused on Mary's influence in our lives [972].

Because she is the mother of Jesus, Mary is the mother of God. As Vatican II puts it: "The Virgin Mary, who at the message of the angel received the Word of God in her heart and in her body and gave Life to the world, is acknowledged and honored as being truly the Mother of God and of the redeemer" (*The Church,* 53) [484-507, 966].

As Mother of the Lord, Mary is an entirely unique person. Like her Son, she was conceived as a human being (and lived her whole life) exempt from any trace of original sin. This is called her *Immaculate Conception* [490-493, 508].

Before, during, and after the birth of her son, Mary remained physically a virgin [510-511]. At the end of her life, Mary was assumed—that is, taken up—body and soul into heaven. This is called her *Assumption* [966].

As Mother of the Christ whose life we live, Mary is also the Mother of the whole Church. She is a member of the Church, but an altogether unique member. Vatican II expresses her relationship to us as "pre-eminent and as a wholly unique member of the Church, and as its type and outstanding model in faith and charity....The Catholic Church taught by the Holy Spirit, honors her with filial affection and devotion as a most beloved mother" (*The Church*, 53) [971].

Like a mother waiting up for her grown children to come home, Mary never stops influencing the course of our lives. Vatican II says: "She conceived, brought forth, and nourished Christ, she presented him to the Father in the temple, shared her Son's sufferings as he died on the cross....For this reason she is a mother to us in the order of grace" (*The Church,* 61) [484-507]. "By her maternal charity, she cares for the brethren of her Son, who still journey on earth surrounded by dangers and difficulties, until they are led into their blessed home" (*The Church,* 62) [488, 968-970, 2674].

This mother, who saw her own flesh-and-blood son die for the rest of her children, is waiting and preparing your home for you. She is, in the words of Vatican II, your "sign of certain hope and comfort" (*The Church,* 68).

The Church also honors the other saints who are already with the Lord in heaven. These are people who have served God and their neighbors in so outstanding a way that they have been canonized. That is, the Church has officially declared that they are in heaven, holds them up as heroic

31

models, and encourages us to pray to them, asking their intercession with God for us all [956, 957, 962].

10. The Scriptures and Tradition
[80-83]

The Second Vatican Council describes sacred Tradition and sacred Scripture as being "like a mirror, in which the Church, during its pilgrim journey here on earth, contemplates God" (*Revelation,* 7) [97].

God's Word of revelation comes to you through words spoken and written by human beings. "Sacred Scripture is the speech of God as it is put down in writing under the breath of the Holy Spirit" (*Revelation,* 9). Sacred Tradition is the handing on of God's Word by the successors of the apostles. Together, Tradition and Scripture "make up a single sacred deposit of the Word of God, which is entrusted to the Church" (*Revelation,* 10) [95, 97].

The Bible: Its Books and Its Message
[101-141]

Sacred Scripture, the Bible, is a collection of books. According to the canon of Scripture (the Catholic Church's list of books accepted as authentic), the Bible contains 73 books. The 46 books of the Old Testament were written approximately between 900 B.C. and 160 B.C.— that is, before the coming of Christ. The 27 books of the New Testament were written approximately between A.D. 50 and A.D. 140 [120].

The Old Testament collection is made up of historical books, didactic (teaching) books, and prophetic books (containing the inspired words of prophets, people who experienced God in special ways and were his authentic spokesmen). These books, with a few exceptions, were written originally in Hebrew [121].

In brief, the Old Testament books are a record of the experience the Israelite people had of Yahweh, the God of their fathers. (Recall Exodus 3:13-15.) As a whole, these books reveal Israel's insight into the personal reality of the one God, Yahweh, who acts in human history guiding it with plan and purpose. Yahweh, the God of the Old Testament, is the same God whom Jesus, a Jew, called Father [122, 123, 128-130, 140].

The New Testament books, written originally in Greek, are made up of gospels (proclamations of the Good News) and epistles (letters). First, in the order in which they appear in the Bible, are the Gospels of Matthew, Mark, Luke, and John. The first three gospels are called *Synoptic* (from the Greek *synoptikos*, "seeing the whole together") because they tell much the same story in much the same way. The book called Acts of the Apostles, which follows the Gospel of John, is a sequel to the Gospel of Luke; written by Luke, Acts continues the narrative of his Gospel. The Gospel of John (also called the fourth gospel) fills out the view of Jesus found in the three Synoptic Gospels [125-127].

Next in sequence come the epistles of Saint Paul—the earliest New Testament documents—which were written in each case to meet particular needs of various local Christian communities.

After Paul's epistles come the Catholic epistles. These letters are called catholic, or universal, because they were not written to deal with particular needs of local churches but with matters important to all Christian communities.

The final book of the New Testament is the Book of Revelation, a message of hope for persecuted Christians, promising Christ's ultimate triumph in history [120].

The basic theme of the New Testament is Jesus Christ. Each book reveals a different side of his mystery. The four gospels record the words and deeds of Jesus as they were remembered and handed down in the early generations of the Church [139]. They tell the story of his passion and death, and what that death means in the light of his Resurrection. In a sense the gospels *began* with the Resurrection; Jesus' teachings and the events in his life made sense to the early Christians only *after* his Resurrection [638-658]. The gospels reflect the shared faith of the first Christians in the Lord who is risen and now dwells among us [124-127].

The New Testament writings tell not who Jesus *was* but who he *is*. More than mere historical documents, these writings have the power to change your life. In the New Testament "mirror" you can find Jesus Christ. If you accept what you see in that mirror, the meaning Christ has for you in your life situation, you can also find yourself [101-104, 124].

33

Tradition, Vatican II, and Parents
[74-83, 4-10, 1653-1658]

Sacred Tradition is the handing on of God's Word. This handing on is done officially by the successors of the apostles and unofficially by all who worship, teach, and live the faith as the Church understands it [173].

Certain ideas and customs grow out of the Tradition process and become instrumental to it, some even for a period of centuries. But a product of Tradition is a basic element in it only if that product has served to hand on the Faith in an unvarying form since the early centuries of the Church. Examples of basic elements are the Bible (as a tangible tool used in handing on the Faith), the Apostles' Creed, and the basic forms of the Church's liturgy.

In a particular era a product of the Tradition process can play a special role in handing on the faith [74-83]. The documents of ecumenical councils are prime examples. An ecumenical council is an official meeting, for the purpose of decision making, by the bishops of the world who are in union with the pope. The teachings of an ecumenical council—products of Tradition in the strict sense—play a decisive role in the Tradition process [884]. The documents of the sixteenth-century Council of Trent have played such a role. So have the documents of Vatican I, which took place in the nineteenth century [9].

In our time the documents of Vatican II are playing the same role in the handing-on process. As Pope Paul VI declared in a 1966 address: "We must give thanks to God and have confidence in the future of the Church when we think of the Council: it will be *the great catechism of our times*" [10].

Vatican II has done what the teaching Church has always done: it has spelled out the unchangeable content of revelation, translating it into thought-forms of people in today's culture. But this "translation of unchangeable content" is not just old news dressed up in new language. As Vatican II has stated: "The Tradition that comes from the apostles makes progress in the Church, with the help of the Holy Spirit. There is a *growth* in insight into the realities and words that are being passed on....As the centuries go by, the Church is always advancing towards the plenitude of divine truth, until eventually the words of God are fulfilled in her" (*Revelation*, 8) [77-79, 98, 2650, 2651].

Through Vatican II the Church has heeded the Spirit and engaged in its "responsibility of reading the signs of the time and of interpreting them in the light of the Gospel" (*Church in the Modern World,* 4). Where the Spirit is leading us is not always clear. But the ground on which we the Church move forward in our pilgrimage is firm: the Gospel of Christ. At this stage in our history, one of our basic instruments of Tradition—the handing on of the faith—is the documents of Vatican II [767, 768, 810].

Tradition is an entirely personal process. The faith is handed on *by people to people.* Popes and bishops, priests and religious, theologians and teachers, pass on the faith. But the main people involved in the process are parents and their children. Children of Chinese parents seldom develop an Irish brogue. And children of nonreligious parents seldom develop a deep, living faith. So in regard to Tradition, keep in mind the words of the noted English priest-educator, Canon Drinkwater: "You educate to some extent...by what you say, more by what you do, and still more by what you are; but most of all by the things you love" [4-10, 902, 1653-1658, 2204-2206].

11. Sin: Original and Personal

[396-409]

The Original Sin and Its Effects

In its *Pastoral Constitution on the Church in the Modern World,* Vatican II states: "Although set by God in a state of rectitude, man, enticed by the evil one, abused his freedom at the very start of history. He lifted himself up against God, and sought to attain his goal apart from him" (13) [397].

In narrative form, chapters 1 through 11 of the Book of Genesis depict this somber fact about humankind. Chapters 1 and 2 of Genesis tell the story of creation by God. God created all things, including man and woman, and saw that they were good [279-324, 355-384].

But into this good world entered sin. In chapter 3 of Genesis, the man, Adam, rejects God and tries to become his equal. As a result of this original sin, the man feels alienated from God. He hides. When God confronts him, Adam blames the woman, Eve, for his sin, and she in turn blames the serpent. The point is simple and tragic: the man's guilt has distorted all his relationships. Sin has turned life into a harsh burden [385, 397-401].

Chapters 4 through 11 of Genesis depict the escalation of sin in the world, rippling out from Adam's original sin. Cain murders his brother Abel. Sin reaches such proportions that God sends a great flood that covers the earth—a symbol of the chaos and destruction sin brought to creation. In chapter 11 human folly reaches its peak: man tries again to become God's equal by building a tower reaching to the heavens [56, 57, 60]. This rejection of God spills over into man's rejection of his fellowman. There is now division and complete lack of communication among nations [1865].

According to Genesis, a world of beauty was deformed by sin. The ongoing result has been division, pain, bloodshed, loneliness, and death. This tragic narrative has a familiar feel to it. The reality it points to is a basic part of human experience. It is no surprise that this reality—the fact of original sin and its effects—is a teaching of the Church [396-409].

With the exception of Jesus Christ and his Mother Mary, every human being born into this world is affected by original sin. As Saint Paul declared in Romans 5:12, "Therefore, just as through one person sin entered the world, and through sin, death, and thus death came to all, inasmuch as all sinned" [402].

While continuing to point out that there is evil in this world, the Church does not suggest that human nature is corrupt. Rather, humankind is capable of much good. While experiencing a "downward pull," we still maintain essential control over our decisions. Free will remains [386-390]. And—most importantly—Christ our Redeemer has conquered sin and death by his death and resurrection. This victory has swallowed up not only our personal sins but the original sin and its widespread effects. The doctrine of original sin, then, is best viewed as a dark backdrop against which can be contrasted the brilliant redemption won for us by Christ our Lord [606-618].

Personal Sin

In addition to the effects of original sin, there is personal sin—sin committed by an individual. We sin personally whenever we knowingly and deliberately violate the moral law. By sinning, we fail to love God. We turn aside from—or even back away from—our lifetime goal of doing God's will [1849-1853].

A mortal sin is a fundamental rejection of God's love. By it, God's grace-presence is driven from the sinner. *Mortal* means "death-dealing." This sin kills God's life and love in the person sinning. For a sin to be mortal, there must be (1) serious matter, (2) sufficient reflection, and (3) full consent of the will [1854-1861].

A venial sin is a less serious rejection of God's love. *Venial* means "easily forgiven." A sin is venial if the offense is not serious or—if the matter is serious—the person is not sufficiently aware of the evil involved or does not fully consent to the sin.

Venial sin is like a spiritual sickness that hurts but does not kill God's grace-presence within the person. There can be degrees of seriousness in sinning just as different sicknesses can be more or less serious. Even less serious sins, however, should not be taken lightly. People in love do not want to offend one another in any way, even the slightest [1862, 1863].

Sins, of whatever seriousness, do not have to be actions. A person can sin by thought or desire or by failing to do something that should be done [1849, 1871].

God will forgive any sin—even the most serious—over and over if the person is truly sorry [1864].

A person who judges himself or herself to be in mortal sin must be reconciled to Christ and the Church before he or she receives holy Communion [1385]. (See 1 Corinthians 11:27-28.) A person in mortal sin can return to God's grace before confession by having perfect sorrow or contrition, but this perfect contrition must be accompanied by the intention to confess the sin and receive sacramental absolution [1452, 1455, 1456].

Personal Sin and Social Evil
[1865-1869]

Patterns of evil can be institutionalized. Injustice, for example, can become part of a group's way of life, embedded in laws and social customs. Such patterns, in a ripple effect, contaminate the attitudes and actions of people in that environment. The influence of these patterns can be so subtle that people enmeshed in them may literally be unaware of the evil they promote [1865-1869].

The mystery of original sin has a social dimension, and cooperation in evil patterns deepens the presence of evil in the world. It contributes to human suffering. Thus, Vatican II makes a point of focusing—especially during the penitential season of Lent—on "the social consequences of sin" (*The Constitution on the Sacred Liturgy,* 109).

To go along with institutional evil makes a person "part of the problem"—an active descendant of the Old Man, Adam. To resist or confront social evil makes you "part of the answer"—a person alive with the life won for us by the New Man, Jesus Christ [1869, 1872].

Formation of a Correct Conscience
[1776-1802]

Speaking out for the dignity of human beings, Vatican II says: "Deep within his conscience man discovers a law which he has not laid upon himself but which he must obey. Its voice, ever calling him to love and to do what is good and to avoid evil, tells him inwardly at the right moment: do this, shun that. For man has in his heart a law inscribed by God. His dignity lies in observing this law, and by it he will be judged. His conscience is man's most secret core, and his sanctuary. There he is alone with God whose voice echoes in his depths" (*Church in the Modern World,* 16) [1777-1782].

We are all morally bound to follow our conscience. But this does not mean that what our conscience tells us is infallibly correct. As Vatican II says, "Conscience goes astray through ignorance" (16)—that is, from ignorance for which a person is not morally responsible. Seeking a correct conscience is part of our dignity and responsibility [1790-1794].

Speaking of a correct conscience, Vatican II states: "Hence, the more a correct conscience prevails, the more do persons and groups turn aside from blind choice and try to be guided by the objective standards of moral conduct" (*Church in the Modern World,* 16) [1786-1789].

Regarding the crucial matter of how to develop a right conscience, the Council says: "In forming their consciences the faithful must pay careful attention to the sacred and certain teaching of the Church. For the Catholic Church is by the will of Christ the teacher of truth. It is her duty to proclaim and teach with authority the truth which is Christ and, at the same time, to declare and confirm by her authority the principles of the moral order which spring from human nature itself" (*Declaration on Religious Liberty,* 14). In personal matters of conscience, "carefully attend to the sacred and certain teaching of the Church." Then, in the "most secret core and sanctuary" of your heart where you are "alone with God," seek his will. Seek and you will find [1783-1785, 2822, 2823].

12. The Sacraments of the Church

[1210-1666]

Baptism: New Life and Ways of Living

[1210-1284]

Through symbolic immersion in the waters of baptism, you are "grafted into the paschal mystery of Christ." In a mysterious way, you "die with him, are buried with him, and rise with him" (*Sacred Liturgy,* 6) [1086].

As a baptized Christian, you are an adopted brother or sister of Christ, "hid with Christ in God," but a visible member of his Body [1266].

Having died to sin (both original sin and personal sins are cleansed away in the waters of baptism) [1263, 1264], you have entered the community of the Church "as through a door." Your indelible baptism into Christ was the beginning of a unique lifelong vocation [1214-1216, 1263, 1271].

Many people exercise their baptismal calling through parish activi-ties. Assisting their parish priests, they serve as distributors of holy Communion, lectors, commentators, choir leaders, ushers, servers, members of the parish council, the Legion of Mary, the St. Vincent de Paul Society, the Holy Name Society, and many other parish groups [911].

Some serve the spiritual and community life of their parishes by teaching religion and taking part in adult-education programs, Scripture study, prayer groups, and family enrichment groups, such as Marriage Encounter. Many find their baptismal faith revitalized by praising God together as charmismatic Catholics. These are only some of the ways in which baptized members of Christ's Body live out the mystery of their baptismal vocation [898-913].

A major way of living the life of baptism is called the religious life. Heeding a special grace from God, some people enter religious orders and congregations and become religious Brothers and Sisters [914-933, 944, 945]. (Some religious also become priests, blending their religious life with their special priestly ministry.)

As consecrated religious, these people dedicate themselves to God by vowing to live the evangelical counsels of poverty, chastity, and obedience. As Vatican II explains, their lives are devoted to God's service: "This constitutes a special consecration, which is deeply rooted in their baptismal consecration and is a fuller expression of it" (*Decree on the Up-to-Date Renewal of Religious Life,* 5)[930, 944, 2102, 2103].

Through your baptism, you share with others "the sacramental bond of unity existing among all who through it are reborn" (*Decree on Ecumenism,* 22). Your baptism can never be repeated because it binds you to God forever. The bond is unbreakable. It is possible for you to lose grace and even faith, but you cannot lose your baptism. You are marked as one of God's own. That same bond links you to all other baptized persons in a sacramental way. You are one of us and we are all "sacrament persons." Together we are called to live until death the baptismal mystery into which we have been plunged [941, 1271, 2791].

Confirmation: Seal of the Spirit, Gift of the Father
[1285-1321]

Confirmation is the sacrament by which those born anew in baptism receive the seal of the Holy Spirit, the Gift of the Father. Along with

40

baptism and the Eucharist, confirmation is sacrament of initiation—in this case, initiation into the life of adult Christian witness. The deepened presence of the Spirit, who comes to us in this sacrament, is meant to sustain us in a lifetime of witness to Christ and service to others [1302, 1303].

If you were being confirmed today, the celebrant would moisten his thumb with chrism, the specially blessed mixture of olive oil and balsam, and trace the sign of the cross on your forehead. This act is the laying on of hands, which is an actual part of the sacrament going back to the time of the apostles.

While anointing you, the celebrant would address you, using your new confirmation name, and say: "Be sealed with the Gift of the Holy Spirit." These words have rich connections with early Christianity. As Saint Paul wrote to the Christians in Ephesus, "In him you also...were sealed with the promised holy Spirit, which is the first installment of our inheritance..." (Ephesians 1:13-14) [1299, 1300].

The word *Gift*, used in confirmation, is spelled with a capital, because the Gift we receive in this sacrament is the Spirit himself [1293].

Eucharist: Sacrifice and Sacrament
[1322-1419]

In its *Constitution on the Sacred Liturgy,* Vatican II begins chapter 2, "The Most Sacred Mystery of the Eucharist," with these beautiful words:

"At the Last Supper, on the night when he was betrayed, our Savior instituted the eucharistic sacrifice of his Body and Blood. This he did in order to perpetuate the sacrifice of the Cross throughout the ages until he should come again, and so to entrust to his beloved Spouse, the Church, a memorial of his death and resurrection: a sacrament of love, a sign of unity, a bond of charity, a paschal banquet in which Christ is consumed, the mind is filled with grace, and a pledge of future glory is given to us" (47) [1323, 1398].

This mystery is the very center and culmination of Christian life. It is the "source and the summit of all preaching of the Gospel...the center of the assembly of the faithful" (*Life of Priests*, 5) [1175, 1181, 1324, 1392].

In every Mass, Christ is present, both in the person of his priest and especially under the form of bread and wine. In every Mass, his death becomes a present reality, offered as our sacrifice to God in an unbloody and sacramental manner. As often as the sacrifice of the cross is celebrated on an altar, the work of our redemption is carried on [1333, 1350, 1372].

At Mass we offer Christ, our passover sacrifice, to God, and we offer ourselves along with him. We then receive the risen Lord, our bread of life, in holy Communion. In so doing, we enter into the very core of the paschal mystery of our salvation—the death and resurrection of Christ [1330, 1356-1359].

Eating the supper of the Lord, we span all time and "proclaim the death of the Lord until he comes" (1 Corinthians 11:26). Sharing this banquet of love, we become totally one body in him. At that moment our future with God becomes a present reality. The oneness for which we are destined is both symbolized and made real in the meal we share. In the Mass, both past and future become really present in mystery [1382-1398, 1402, 1405].

If you prepare for it with care and enter into it with living faith, the Eucharist can draw you into the compelling love of Christ and set you afire. When you go out from the sacred mystery, you know you were caught up in it if you "grasp by deed what you hold by creed." And if you return to the place where the Blessed Sacrament is kept, Christ present in the tabernacle, you can regain your sense of the fathomless love his presence there silently speaks [1066-1075, 1418].

Penance: Reconciliation
[1422-1498]

Penance is the sacrament by which we receive God's healing forgiveness for sins committed after baptism. The rite is called reconciliation because it reconciles us not only with God but with the Church community. Both these aspects of reconciliation are important [1468-1470].

As members of Christ's Body, everything we do affects the whole Body. Sin wounds and weakens the Body of Christ; the healing we receive in penance restores health and strength to the Church, as well as to ourselves.

When a person turns aside or away from God's love, the harm is to the sinner. Venial sin strains one's relationship with God. Mortal sin ruptures the relationship [1854-1863].

Sin is a tragic reality. But the sacrament of penance is a joyful reunion. Chapter 15 of Luke's Gospel expresses this joy poignantly: the Pharisees accuse Jesus of being too merciful. In response, Jesus tells three parables. In the first, God is like a shepherd who leaves ninety-nine sheep to seek one who is lost. When he finds it, he is filled with joy [1443].

In the second parable, a woman finds a valuable coin she had lost and throws a big party. Jesus comments: "In just the same way, I tell you, there will be rejoicing among the angels of God over one sinner who repents" (15:10) [545-546].

The third parable is the story of the wayward son. When the son returns home, his father receives him with a tender embrace [2839].

When you confess your sins sincerely, with true sorrow and resolution not to sin again, God rejoices. The Pharisees depicted in Luke's Gospel were stern, rigid men—stricter judges than God. In contrast, the Father revealed by Jesus is almost too good to be true. And so is Jesus himself, whom you meet in this sacrament. Like Father, like Son. In penance, Jesus embraces and heals you [1441-1442].

Anointing of the Sick
[1499-1532]

In serious illness you experience mortality. You realize that at some time *you* are going to die. If you are not seriously ill, but infirm or aged, you know this same experience.

Because these circumstances lead you to face God in the light of your own death, there is something especially sacramental about the condition you are in. And so there is a formal sacrament for this sacramental situation: anointing of the sick [1522].

Anointing does not hasten the act of death. In this sacrament, however, God does invite you to commune with him in the light of your final meeting with him. Through this sacrament, the entire Church asks God to lighten your sufferings, forgive your sins, and bring you to eternal salvation [1520].

You need not be on the verge of dying to receive this sacrament. This is clear from the fact that the anointing and the prayers that accompany it have as a purpose the restoration of health. Therefore, if you are not in immediate danger of death, but are infirm or aged, you can and should ask for the sacrament. If you ever are in danger of death, either from sickness or old age, you should not delay receiving the sacrament [1514-1515].

Anointing of the sick helps you to share more fully in the cross of Christ. By so sharing, you contribute to the spiritual good of the whole Church. By the fact that you share more fully in the cross of Christ through anointing, you are being prepared for a fuller share in Christ's Resurrection [1521].

Holy Orders: Ministerial Priesthood
[1536-1600]

The Church is the Body of Christ. As such, the whole Church shares in the nature and tasks of Christ, our head. This includes sharing in his priesthood [787-796, 1268, 1546].

But beyond this "common priesthood of the faithful," there is the special or "ministerial priesthood" of Christ that certain members of the Church receive through the sacrament of holy orders [901, 1547].

Each type of priesthood—common or ministerial—is a sharing in the priesthood of Christ. And both types are related to each other. But there is a basic difference between them. In the eucharistic sacrifice, for example, the ordained priest acts "in the person of Christ" and offers the sacrifice to God in the name of all, and the people join with the priest in that offering. The two roles—of priest and people—go together [901-903].

Priests receive their priesthood from bishops, who possess the fullness of the sacrament of holy orders. When a bishop ordains priests, he gives them a sharing of his priesthood and mission [1562-1564].

Priests share in Christ's ministry by preaching his gospel, doing all in their power to bring their people to Christian maturity. They baptize, heal, forgive sin in the sacrament of penance, and act as the Church's witness in the sacraments of matrimony and anointing of the sick. Most importantly, priests celebrate the Eucharist, which is "the center of the assembly of the faithful over which the priest presides" (*Decree on the Ministry and Life of Priests*, 5). All priests are united in the single goal of building up Christ's Body [1565-1568, 1595].

When priests are ordained, they "are signed with a special character," an interior capability that empowers them to "act in the person of Christ the head" (*Life of Priests*, 2). This special inner "character" unites priests in a sacramental bond with one another—a fact that, in a sense, sets them apart from other people. This "being set apart" is meant to help priests do God's work with total dedication [1581-1584].

As Vatican II points out, priests "exercise other services for the benefit of men [and women]" just as Jesus did (*Life of Priests*, 2). One thing this means is that priests need their people just as their people need them. Laypeople who work closely with priests help them to be leaders in the community of God's people [910].

In addition to bishops and priests, deacons also have a special sharing in the sacrament of holy orders. The diaconate, conferred by a bishop, is received as the first stage in ordination by those who go on to the priesthood. Since the Second Vatican Council, however, the ancient order of deacon has been restored in the Roman Catholic Church as an office in its own right. Many dioceses now have deacons who do not go on to become priests. They are known, therefore, as *permanent* deacons. Working under the authority of the local bishop, permanent deacons serve the people of God at the direction of priests in parishes [1569-1571, 1596].

Matrimony: Sacrament of Life-Giving Oneness
[1601-1666]

In all civilizations people have sensed a mysterious sacredness about the union of man and woman. There has always been a vague realization that the deep longing for oneness with "the other" is life-giving—and that it is a longing for oneness with the source of all life. This is why religious rituals and codes of behavior have always been connected with marriage.

Jesus made marriage the sacrament of matrimony, giving matrimony a new dimension to the Christian vocation that begins in baptism [1601].

In matrimony a husband and wife are called to love each other in a very practical way: by serving each other's most personal needs; by working seriously at communicating their personal thoughts and feelings to each other so their oneness is always alive and growing. This love is explicitly, beautifully sexual. As Vatican II points out, "Married love is uniquely expressed and perfected by the exercise of the acts proper to marriage" (*Church in the Modern World,* 49) [1643-1654].

In matrimony a couple is also called to live their sacrament for others. By their obvious closeness, a couple affects the lives of others with "something special"—the love of Christ in our midst. They reveal Christ's love and make it contagious to their children and to all who come into contact with them. A major purpose and natural outcome of matrimony is the begetting of new life—children. But a couple's love also gives life—the life of Christ's Spirit—to other people [1652-1658, 2366, 2367].

A couple does not live a life of love because they happen to be compatible. They do it consciously and deliberately because it is their vocation and because matrimony is called "a great mystery…in reference to Christ and the church" (Ephesians 5:32) [1616].

Matrimony is much more than a private arrangement between two people. It is a sacramental vocation in and for the Church. It is a medium through which Christ reveals and deepens the mystery of his oneness with us, his Body. Thus, husbands and wives live a truly sacramental life when they follow the advice given in Ephesians 5:21: "Be subordinate to one another out of reverence for Christ" [1617].

In the Catholic Church, a couple's sacramental union is *exclusive* (one man with one woman) and *indissoluble* (till death do us part). These are concrete ways in which the mysterious oneness between husband and wife, Christ and Church, becomes reality [1643-1645, 2360-2379].

The best thing parents can do for their children is to love each other. Similarly, one of the best things a couple can do for the Church and for the world is to strive for greater closeness [2201-2231].

13. Human Destiny

[988-1060]

Individual Death and Judgment

The Church believes in two final destinies—one for individuals and one for humankind as a whole [678-679].

What you can expect at death is expressed in the New Testament Letter to the Hebrews. It says, "It is appointed that human beings die once, and after this the judgment…" (9:27) [1013, 1021].

Your life as an earthly pilgrim reaches its point of arrival at the moment of death. Having passed beyond the world of time and change, you can no longer choose a different reality as the ultimate love of your life. If your basic love-choice at the moment of death was the absolute Good whom we call God, God remains your eternal possession. This eternal possession of God is called heaven [1023-1029].

If your ultimate love-choice at the moment of death was anything less than God, you experience the radical emptiness of not possessing the absolute Good. This eternal loss is called hell [1033-1037, 1056, 1057].

The judgment at the instant of death consists in a crystal-clear revelation of your unchangeable, freely chosen condition—eternal union with God, or eternal alienation [1021, 1022].

Purgatory and the Communion of Saints
[1030-1032, 954-959]

If you die in the love of God but possess any "stains of sin," such stains are cleansed away in a purifying process called purgatory. These stains of sin are primarily the temporal punishment due to venial or mortal sins already forgiven but for which sufficient penance was not done during your lifetime. This doctrine of purgatory, reflected in Scripture and developed in Tradition, was clearly expressed in the Second Council of Lyons (A.D. 1274).

Having passed through purgatory, you will be utterly unselfish, capable of perfect love. Your selfish ego—that part of you that restlessly sought self-satisfaction—will have died forever. The "new you" will be your same inner self, transformed and purified by the intensity of God's love for you.

Besides declaring the fact of purgatory, the Second Council of Lyons also affirmed that "the faithful on earth can be of great help" to persons undergoing purgatory by offering for them "the sacrifice of the Mass, prayers, almsgiving, and other religious deeds" [958, 1032, 1055].

Implied in this doctrine is the bond of oneness—called the communion of saints—that exists between the people of God on earth and those who have gone before us. Vatican II focuses on this bond of union by saying that it "accepts loyally the venerable faith of our ancestors in the living communion which exists between us and our brothers who are in the glory of heaven or who are yet being purified after their death" (*The Church,* 51) [828, 959].

The communion of saints is a two-way street. In the section quoted above, Vatican II points out that just as you on earth can help those who undergo purgatory, those in heaven can help you on your pilgrimage by interceding with God [946-962].

Hell
[1033-1037]

God, who is infinite love and mercy, is also infinite justice [1040]. Because of God's justice, as well as his total respect for human freedom, hell is a real possibility as a person's eternal destiny. This side of God's mystery is difficult for us to grasp. But Christ himself taught it, and so does the Church [1861].

The teaching on hell is clearly in Scripture. In the Gospel of Matthew, Christ says to the just: "Come, you who are blessed by my Father. Inherit the kingdom prepared for you from the foundation of the world." But to the unjust he says: "Depart from me, you accursed, into the eternal fire prepared for the devil and his angels" (25:34, 41). Elsewhere, Jesus is recorded as saying: "It is better for you to enter into life maimed than with two hands to go into Gehenna" (Mark 9:43) [1056, 1057].

One point that emerges quite clearly from this doctrine is the reality of human freedom. You are free to seek God and serve him. And you are free to do the opposite. In either case you are responsible for the consequences. Life is a serious matter. The way you live it makes a serious difference. You are free, radically free, to seek God. And you are free, radically free, to choose the inexpressible pain of his absence [1730-1748].

Heaven
[1023-1029]

Grace, God's presence within you, is like a seed—a vital, growing seed that is destined one day to break forth full grown.

God has given himself to you, but in a hidden way. For the time being, you seek him even as you possess him. But the time will come when your seeking will be over. You will then see and possess God completely. This has been revealed [1024].

In his First Letter, Saint John says: "Beloved, we are God's children now; what we shall be has not yet been revealed. We do know that when it is revealed we shall be like him, for we shall see him as he is" (3:2) [1720].

And in his First Letter to the Corinthians, Saint Paul says: "At present we see indistinctly, as in a mirror, but then face to face. At present I know partially; then I shall know fully, as I am fully known" (13:12) [164].

This is heaven: direct face-to-face vision of God as he is—Father, Son, and Spirit; total and perfect union with God, an ecstasy of fulfillment beyond human imagining; the "now" of eternity in which everything is ever new, fresh, and present to you; the warm flood of joy in the company of Jesus, his Mother, and all those you have ever known and loved; a total absence of pain, regret, bad memories; the perfect enjoyment of all your powers of mind and (after the resurrection on Judgment Day) of body.

This is heaven. That is to say, this is a pale, human indication of what God has promised to those who love him, of what Christ has gained for us by his death and resurrection [163, 1023, 1024, 2519].

A New Earth and a New Heaven
[1042-1050]

Belief in the Final Judgment on the last day is clearly expressed in the Creeds of the Church. On that day all the dead will be raised. Through divine power, we will all be present before God as bodily human beings [681, 682]. Then God—the absolute Lord of history—will conduct a panoramic judgment of all that humankind did and endured through the long centuries in which the Spirit struggled to bring us forth as one people [1038-1041].

When will that day come? In a remarkable passage filled with hope for all things human, Vatican II addresses this question and expresses the Church's vision: "We know neither the moment of the consummation of the earth and of man nor the way the universe will be transformed. The form of this world, distorted by sin, is passing away and we are taught that God is preparing a new dwelling and a new earth in which righteousness dwells, whose happiness will fill and surpass all the desires of peace arising in the hearts of men" (*Church in the Modern World,* 39) [1001, 1048, 1059, 1060].

Meanwhile, during the time that is left to us, "the body of a new human family grows, foreshadowing in some way the age which is to come" (*Church in the Modern World,* 39) [1049, 2820].

After we have "spread on earth the fruits of our nature and our enterprise—human dignity, brotherly communion, and freedom—according to the command of the Lord and in his Spirit, we will find them once again, cleansed this time from the stain of sin, illuminated and transfigured….Here on earth the kingdom is mysteriously present; when the Lord comes it will enter into its perfection" (*Church in the Modern World,* 39) [1048-1050].

That kingdom is already present in mystery. The day has already begun when God "will wipe every tear from their eyes, and there shall be no more death or mourning." The day has already begun when he says to all living things: "Behold, I make all things new….They are accomplished. I [am] the Alpha and the Omega, the beginning and the end" (Revelation 21:4, 5, 6) [1044, 1186].

Meanwhile, we work and pray for the full flowering of that kingdom to come. With the early Christians, we cry out: *Marana tha!* Come, Lord Jesus! We seek you [1130, 1403, 2548-2550, 2853].

SECTION TWO
PRACTICES

1. God's Two Great Commandments
[Book III, Part 2]

The basis of all law (your rule of life) rests on two commandments: "You shall love the Lord, your God, with all your heart, with all your soul, and with all your mind....You shall love your neighbor as yourself" (Matthew 22:37, 39) [2055, 2083].

2. Commandments of God
[2084-2557]

These are an extension of the two great commandments. The first three tell you how to love your God; the rest show you how to love your neighbor [2196].

1. You shall honor no other god but me [2084-2141].
2. You shall not misuse the name of the Lord your God [2142-2167].
3. Remember to keep holy the Sabbath [2168-2195].
4. Honor your father and your mother [2197-2257].
5. You shall not kill [2258-2330].
6. You shall not commit adultery [2331-2400].
7. You shall not steal [2401-2463].
8. You shall not bear false witness against your neighbor [2464-2513].
9. You shall not covet your neighbor's wife [2514-2533].
10. You shall not covet your neighbor's goods [2534-2557].

3. Precepts of the Church

[2041-2043, 2048]

From time to time, the Church has listed certain specific duties of Catholics. Some duties expected of Catholic Christians today include the following. (Those traditionally mentioned as Precepts of the Church are marked with an asterisk.)

1. To keep holy the day of the Lord's Resurrection: to worship God by participating in Mass every Sunday and every holy day of obligation: * to avoid those activities that would hinder renewal of soul and body, for example, needless work and business activities, unnecessary shopping, and so forth [1166, 1167, 1389, 2042, 2174-2192].
2. To lead a sacramental life: to receive holy Communion frequently and the sacrament of penance regularly
   —minimally, to receive the sacrament of penance at least once a year (annual confession is obligatory only if serious sin is involved) [1389, 2042]. * (See explanation on pages 54 and 55.)
   —minimally, to receive holy Communion at least once a year, between the first Sunday of Lent and Trinity Sunday or, for a just cause, at another time during the year [1389, 1417, 2042].
3. To study Catholic teaching in preparation for the sacrament of confirmation, to be confirmed, and then to continue to study and advance the cause of Christ [1309, 1319].
4. To observe the marriage laws of the Church: [1601-1666] * to give religious training (by example and word) to one's children; to use parish schools and religious-education programs [1656, 1657].
5. To strengthen and support the Church: * one's own parish community and parish priests; the worldwide Church and the Holy Father [1351, 2043].
6. To do penance, including abstaining from meat and fasting from food on the appointed days [1438, 2043]. * (See pages 54 and 55.)
7. To join in the missionary spirit and apostolate of the Church [2044-2046].

4. Holy Days of Obligation

[2043, 2180, 2698]

Holy days of obligation are special feasts on which Catholics who have reached the age of reason are seriously obliged, as on Sundays, to assist at Mass and to avoid unnecessary work. Serious reasons excuse us from these obligations. In the United States these days are: Mary, Mother of God, January 1; Ascension Thursday, forty days after Easter; Mary's Assumption, August 15; All Saints' Day, November 1; Mary's Immaculate Conception, December 8; Christmas, December 25 [2180].

(In Canada, Christmas and Mary, Mother of God are holy days. Others formerly specified have either been made nonobligatory or transferred to the following Sunday.)

5. Regulations for Fast and Abstinence

[2043]

"All persons who have completed their fourteenth year are bound by the law of abstinence; all adults are bound by the law of fast up to the beginning of their sixtieth year." ("The completion of the fourteenth year means the day after one's fourteenth birthday. The beginning of the sixtieth year means the obligation ceases at midnight between the fifty-ninth birthday and the next day.") (See Canon Law, 1252.) The law of abstinence forbids the eating of meat. The law of fasting allows only one full meal and two lighter meals in the course of the day and prohibits eating between meals.

In the United States, Ash Wednesday and Good Friday are days of fast and abstinence; all other Fridays of Lent are days of abstinence only. Some form of penance is especially encouraged on all Fridays throughout the year [1438]. (Catholics living in Canada should consult their parish priests about Canadian regulations.)

Pregnant women and people who are sick are not obliged to fast. Others who feel they are unable to observe the laws of fast and abstinence should consult a parish priest or confessor.

Fast and abstinence are recognized forms of penance. By doing these and other penances, we can realize that interior change of heart that is so necessary for all Christians [1434-1437].

6. Confession of Sins

[1424, 1491]

The precept to confess at least once a year is a reminder to receive the sacrament of penance (reconciliation) on a regular basis. If no grave sin has been committed in that time, confession is not necessary [1493]. However, frequent confession is of great value; it makes us more deeply conformed to Christ and most submissive to the voice of the Spirit [2042].

Reconciliation is a personal encounter with Jesus Christ represented by the priest in the confessional or reconciliation room. The penitent admits to God that he or she has sinned, makes an act of sorrow, accepts a penance (prayers, acts of self-denial, or works of service to others), and resolves to do better in the future [983, 986, 1441, 1442].

After prayer and an examination of conscience to find out what sins you have committed, you enter the confessional [1450-1460]. (This new form, although preferable, is optional.)

Father greets you kindly.

You respond and then make and say the Sign of the Cross.

Father invites you to have confidence in God.

You answer, "Amen."

Father may read or recite some short selection from the Bible.

You introduce yourself (not by name) and tell how long it has been since your last confession. You then tell your sins. (Each mortal sin must be confessed as well as possible.) It is useful to mention your most frequent and most troublesome venial sins.

Father will give you any necessary advice and answer your questions. After he assigns a penance *you* make an Act of Contrition (see page 64).

Father then places his hands on your head (or extends his right hand toward you) and prays these words of forgiveness:

God, the Father of mercies, through the death and resurrection of his Son has reconciled the world to himself and sent the Holy

Spirit among us for the forgiveness of sins; through the ministry of the Church may God give you pardon and peace, and I absolve you from your sins in the name of the Father, and of the Son, and of the Holy Spirit.

You answer, "Amen."
Father then says, "Give thanks to the Lord, for he is good."
You answer, "His mercy endures for ever."
Father then dismisses you in these or similar words, "The Lord has freed you from your sins. Go in peace."
(For further information on penance, read page 41.)

7. Regulations for the Communion Fast
[1387, 1415]

The conditions for receiving holy Communion are the state of grace (freedom from mortal sin), the right intention (not out of routine or human respect but for the purpose of pleasing God), and observance of the Communion fast.

This fast means that you must not eat anything or drink any liquid (other than water) one hour before the reception of Communion. However, the sick and aged, even those not confined to bed or a home (and those caring for them who wish to receive Communion but cannot fast for an hour without inconvenience), can receive holy Communion *even if they have taken something during the previous hour.*

8. How to Receive Communion
[1384-1390, 1415-1417]

Holy Communion may be received on the tongue or in the hand and may be given under the form of bread alone or under both species [1390].

When the minister of the Eucharist addresses the communicant with the words "The Body of Christ," "The Blood of Christ," the communicant responds "Amen" to each.

When the minister raises the eucharistic bread or wine, this is an invitation for the communicant to make an Act of Faith, to express his or

55

her belief in the Eucharist, to manifest a need and desire for the Lord, to accept the good news of Jesus' paschal mystery.

A clear, meaningful, and purposeful "Amen" is your response to this invitation. In this way, you openly profess your belief in the presence of Christ in the eucharistic bread and wine, as well as in his Body, the Church.

9. Beatitudes

[1716-1717]

Positive Christianity involves more than obedience to laws. Those who follow Christ and live by his Spirit know that their salvation rests on struggle and pain. The beatitudes are a summary of the difficulties to be overcome by faithful Christians and the rewards that will be theirs if they are loyal followers of Christ (Matthew 5:3-10).

1. Blessed are the poor in spirit, / for theirs is the kingdom of heaven [544].
2. Blessed are they who mourn, / for they will be comforted.
3. Blessed are the meek, / for they will inherit the land.
4. Blessed are they who hunger and thirst for righteousness, / for they will be satisfied.
5. Blessed are the merciful, / for they will be shown mercy.
6. Blessed are the clean of heart, / for they will see God [1720, 2518, 2546].
7. Blessed are the peacemakers, / for they will be called children of God [2305, 2306, 2330].
8. Blessed are they who are persecuted for the sake of righteousness, / for theirs is the kingdom of heaven.

Here is a shorter version of the beatitudes.

1. Happy are those who need God.
2. Happy are those with self-control.
3. Happy are those who are sorry for sin.
4. Happy are those who hunger and thirst for holiness.

5. Happy are the merciful.
6. Happy are those who love with all their heart.
7. Happy are the peacemakers.
8. Happy are those who suffer for doing what is right.

10. Corporal (Material) Works of Mercy

[2443, 2447]

1. To feed the hungry.
2. To give drink to the thirsty.
3. To clothe the naked.
4. To visit the imprisoned.
5. To shelter the homeless.
6. To visit the sick.
7. To bury the dead [1681-1690, 2300].

11. Spiritual Works of Mercy

[2443, 2447]

1. To admonish the sinner.
2. To instruct the ignorant.
3. To counsel the doubtful.
4. To comfort the sorrowful.
5. To bear wrongs patiently.
6. To forgive all injuries.
7. To pray for the living and the dead [958, 1032].

or

1. Correct those who need it.
2. Teach the ignorant.
3. Give advice to those who need it.
4. Comfort those who suffer.
5. Be patient with others.
6. Forgive others who hurt you.
7. Pray for others.

12. How to Baptize in Case of an Emergency
[1240-1256, 1284]

Pour ordinary water on the forehead (not the hair) of the person to be baptized and say while pouring it: "I baptize you in the name of the Father, and of the Son, and of the Holy Spirit." (Note: Any person can and should baptize in case of necessity; the same person must say the words while pouring the water.)

13. How to Prepare for a Sick Call
(Reconciliation, Communion, Anointing)
[1517-1519]

(Be sure to call the parish or a priest whenever a relative or friend has become seriously ill. The person does not have to be in danger of death.)

Cover a small table with a cloth. If possible, have the table near the bed or chair of the sick person. A crucifix and a vessel of holy water should be provided as well as candles.

Communion to the sick may be received at any hour. If the sick person cannot receive the Eucharist under the form of bread, it may be given under the form of wine alone. Those who care for the sick may also receive Communion.

When the priest (deacon, eucharistic minister) arrives, lead the minister to the sick person. Leave the room if the sick person wishes to receive the sacrament of penance. After reconciliation is finished, return and join in the prayers.

14. Liturgical Seasons of the Year
[1163-1173]

Through the liturgy, the work of our redemption is exercised. It is "through the liturgy, especially, that the faithful are enabled to express in their lives and manifest to others the mystery of Christ and the real nature of the true Church" (*Sacred Liturgy*, 2). It is "the summit toward which the activity of the Church is directed; it is also the fount from which all her power flows" (*Sacred Liturgy*, 10) [2698].

On appointed days in the course of the year, the Church celebrates the memory of our redemption by Christ. Throughout the year, the entire mystery of Christ is unfolded. The Church does this in sequence during the various seasons of the liturgical year [1166].

Advent: This season begins four weeks (or slightly less) before Christmas [524]. (The Sunday which falls on or closest to November 30 is its starting point.)

Christmas Season: This season lasts from Christmas until the Baptism of the Lord, the Sunday after Epiphany. (The period from the end of Christmas Season until the beginning of Lent belongs to *Ordinary Time*.) [1171]

Lent: The penitential season of Lent lasts forty days, beginning on Ash Wednesday and ending with the Mass of the Lord's Supper on Holy Thursday. The final week is called Holy Week, and the last three days are called the Paschal Triduum [540, 1438].

Easter Season: This season, whose theme is resurrection from sin to the life of grace, lasts fifty days, from Easter to Pentecost [1096, 1168, 1169].

Ordinary Time: This season comprises the thirty-three or thirty-four weeks in the course of the year that celebrate no particular aspect of the mystery of Christ. Instead, the mystery of Christ in all its fullness is celebrated. It includes not only the period between the end of the Christmas Season and the beginning of Lent but also all the Sundays after Pentecost to the last Sunday of the liturgical year (Christ the King) [1166, 1167, 2177].

SECTION THREE
PRAYERS
[2559-2565, 2697-2699]

Introductory Note

According to an ancient definition, prayer is "keeping company with God." Prayer is *you* relating to God in the deepest recesses of your personality. It is you seeking and communing with the living God—responding to him as he has made himself known to you through the teachings of the Church.

As intimately personal as it is, prayer makes use of word formulas. Liturgical prayer—the official community prayer of the Church—uses approved formulas. So does unofficial group prayer. Even in solitary private prayer, traditional formulas can be of great help.

At its most personal, private prayer is spontaneous or impromptu—and sometimes even wordless. Nonetheless, formulas are practical helps for breaking into prayer and expressing faith. For this reason some of the most loved, time-approved formulas of Catholic devotion are offered here—prayers that express the whole range of prayerful attitudes: adoration, thanksgiving, petition, and atonement. Also offered in this section is a suggested method of private meditative prayer [2700-2704].

1. Sign of the Cross
[232-237]

In the name of the Father, and of the Son, and of the Holy Spirit. Amen.
(Said at the beginning and end of prayers.)

2. Our Father

[2759-2865]

Our Father, who art in heaven, hallowed be thy name; thy kingdom come; thy will be done on earth as in heaven. Give us this day our daily bread; and forgive us our trespasses as we forgive those who trespass against us; and lead us not into temptation, but deliver us from evil. (For the kingdom, the power, and the glory are yours, now and for ever.) Amen.

3. Hail Mary

[2676, 2677]

Hail Mary, full of grace. The Lord is with thee. Blessed art thou among women, and blessed is the fruit of thy womb, Jesus. Holy Mary, Mother of God, pray for us sinners, now and at the hour of our death. Amen.

4. Prayer of Praise

[2639-2643]

Glory to the Father, and to the Son, and to the Holy Spirit; as it was in the beginning, is now, and will be for ever. Amen.

5. The Nicene Creed

[198-1065]

We believe in one God, the Father, the Almighty, maker of heaven and earth, of all that is seen and unseen. We believe in one Lord, Jesus Christ, the only Son of God, eternally begotten of the Father, God from God, Light from Light, true God from true God, begotten, not made, one in Being with the Father. Through him all things were made. For us men and for our salvation he came down from heaven: by the power of the Holy Spirit, he was born of the Virgin Mary, and became man. For our sake he was crucified under Pontius Pilate; he suffered, died, and was buried. On the third day he rose again in fulfillment of the Scriptures; he ascended into heaven and is seated at the right hand of the Father. He will come again in glory to judge the living and the dead, and his kingdom will have no end. We believe in the Holy Spirit, the Lord, the giver of life, who proceeds from the Father and the Son. With the Father and the Son he is worshiped and glorified. He has spoken through the Prophets. We believe in one holy catholic and apostolic Church. We acknowledge one baptism for the forgiveness of sins. We look for the resurrection of the dead, and the life of the world to come. Amen.

6. Apostles' Creed

[198-1065]

I believe in God, the Father almighty, creator of heaven and earth. I believe in Jesus Christ, his only Son, our Lord. He was conceived by the power of the Holy Spirit and born of the Virgin Mary. He suffered under Pontius Pilate, was crucified, died, and was buried. He descended to the dead. On the third day he rose again. He ascended into heaven, and is seated at the right hand of the Father. He will come again to judge the living and the dead. I believe in the Holy Spirit, the holy catholic Church, the communion of saints, the forgiveness of sins, the resurrection of the body, and the life everlasting. Amen.

7. Morning Offering

[2659-2660]

Most holy and adorable Trinity, one God in three Persons, I praise you and give you thanks for all the favors you have bestowed on me. Your goodness has preserved me until now. I offer you my whole being and in particular all my thoughts, words, and deeds, together with all the trials I may undergo this day. Give them your blessing. May your divine love animate them and may they serve your greater glory.

I make this morning offering in union with the divine intentions of Jesus Christ who offers himself daily in the holy sacrifice of the Mass, and in union with Mary, his Virgin Mother and our Mother, who was always the faithful handmaid of the Lord. Amen.

or

Almighty God, I thank you for your past blessings. Today I offer myself—whatever I do, say, or think—to your loving care. Continue to bless me, Lord. I make this morning offering in union with the divine intentions of Jesus Christ who offers himself daily in the holy sacrifice of the Mass, and in union with Mary, his Virgin Mother and our Mother, who was always the faithful handmaid of the Lord. Amen.

The following Acts of Faith, Hope, Love, and Contrition serve well for morning and night prayers.

8. Act of Faith

[1814-1816, 2656]

O my God, I firmly believe that you are one God in three divine Persons, Father, Son, and Holy Spirit; I believe that your divine Son became man and died for our sins, and that he will come to judge the living and the dead. I believe these and all the truths which the holy Catholic Church teaches, because you revealed them, who can neither deceive nor be deceived. Amen.

9. Act of Hope

[1817-1821, 2657]

O my God, relying on your infinite goodness and promises, I hope to obtain pardon of my sins, the help of your grace, and life everlasting, through the merits of Jesus Christ, my Lord and Redeemer. Amen.

10. Act of Love

[1822-1829, 2658]

O my God, I love you above all things, with my whole heart and soul, because you are all good and worthy of all my love. I love my neighbor as myself for the love of you. I forgive all who have injured me and I ask pardon of all whom I have injured. Amen.

11. Act of Contrition

[1450-1460]

(a) My God, I am sorry for my sins with all my heart. In choosing to do wrong and failing to do good, I have sinned against you whom I should love above all things. I firmly intend, with your help, to do penance, to sin no more, and to avoid whatever leads me to sin. Our

Savior Jesus Christ suffered and died for us. In his name, my God, have mercy. Amen.

or

(b) O my God, I am sorry for my sins because I have offended you. I know I should love you above all things. Help me to do penance, to do better, and to avoid anything that might lead me to sin. Amen.

or

(c) Any spontaneous and heartfelt prayer that tells God that you are truly sorry for all your sins, that you will mend your ways, and that you firmly intend to avoid what leads to sin is a good Act of Contrition.

12. Come, Holy Spirit (Prayer for Guidance)

[2670-2672]

Come, Holy Spirit.
Response: Fill the hearts of your faithful and make the fire of your love burn within them.
Send forth your spirit and there shall be another creation.
Response: And you shall renew the face of the earth.
Let us pray: O God, you have instructed the hearts of the faithful by the light of the Holy Spirit. Grant that through the same Holy Spirit we may always be truly wise and rejoice in his consolation. Through Christ our Lord. Amen.

13. Angelus

[973, 2617]

The angel of the Lord declared unto Mary.
Response: And she conceived of the Holy Spirit. (Hail Mary)
Behold the handmaid of the Lord.
Response: May it be done unto me according to your word. (Hail Mary)
And the Word was made flesh.
Response: And dwelt among us. (Hail Mary)

Pray for us, O holy Mother of God.

Response: That we may be made worthy of the promises of Christ.

Let us pray: O Lord, it was through the message of an angel that we learned of the Incarnation of Christ, your Son. Pour your grace into our hearts, and by his Passion and cross bring us to the glory of his Resurrection. Through Christ, our Lord. Amen.

14. Queen of Heaven

[972-975, 2617-2622]

(Prayer during the Easter Season instead of Angelus)

Queen of Heaven, rejoice, alleluia.

Response: The Son whom you were privileged to bear, alleluia, has risen as he said, alleluia.

Pray to God for us, alleluia.

Rejoice and be glad, Virgin Mary, alleluia.

Response: For the Lord has truly risen, alleluia.

Let us pray: O God, it was by the Resurrection of your Son, our Lord Jesus Christ, that you brought joy to the world. Grant that through the intercession of the Virgin Mary, his Mother, we may attain the joy of eternal life. Through Christ, our Lord. Amen.

15. Grace Before and Thanksgiving After Meals

[2698]

Bless us, O Lord, and these your gifts, which we are about to receive from your bounty, through Christ, our Lord. Amen.

We give thanks for all your benefits, almighty God, who lives and reigns forever. May the souls of the faithful departed, through the mercy of God, rest in peace. Amen. (Spontaneous prayers may also be used at mealtime.)

16. Memorare

[2673-2675, 2679]

Remember, O most gracious Virgin Mary, that never was it known that anyone who fled to your protection, implored your help, or sought your intercession was left unaided. Inspired with this confidence, I fly to you, O virgin of virgins, my Mother. To you I come, before you I stand, sinful and sorrowful. O Mother of the Word Incarnate, despise not my petitions, but in your mercy, hear and answer me. Amen.

17. Prayer for Vocations

[914-933, 2004]

Jesus, High Priest and Redeemer forever, we beg you to call young men and women to your service as priests and religious. May they be inspired by the lives of dedicated priests, Brothers, and Sisters. Give to parents the grace of generosity and trust toward you and their children so that their sons and daughters may be helped to choose their vocations in life with wisdom and freedom.

Lord, you told us that "the harvest indeed is great but the laborers are few. Pray, therefore, the Lord of the harvest, to send laborers into his harvest." We ask that we may know and follow the vocation to which you have called us. We pray particularly for those called to serve as priests, Brothers, and Sisters; those whom you have called, those you are calling now, and those you will call in the future. May they be open and responsive to the call of serving your people. We ask this through Christ, our Lord. Amen.

18. Prayer to Jesus Christ Crucified

[618]

Behold, my beloved and good Jesus. I cast myself upon my knees in your sight, and with the most fervent desire of my soul I pray and beseech you to impress upon my heart lively sentiments of faith, hope, and charity, with true repentance for my sins and a most firm desire of amendment; while with deep affection and grief of soul I consider within myself and mentally contemplate your five most precious wounds, having before my eyes that which David the prophet long ago spoke about you, my Jesus: "They have pierced my hands and my feet; / I can count all my bones" (Psalm 22:17-18).

19. Mary's Rosary

[971, 1674, 2678, 2708]

The complete rosary is composed of fifteen decades, divided into three distinct parts, each containing five decades. The first part consists of five joyful events in the life of Jesus and Mary, the second part recalls five sorrowful events, and the third part considers five glorious events.

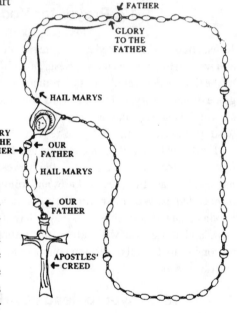

We begin by making the Sign of the Cross.

Then we say the Apostles' Creed, one Our Father, three Hail Marys, and one Glory to the Father (Prayer of Praise) on the small chain. Then recall the first mystery, say one Our Father, ten Hail Marys, and one Glory to the Father. This completes one decade. All the other decades are said in the same manner with a different mystery meditated during each decade. At the end of the rosary, the prayer Hail, Holy Queen may be recited.

The mysteries of the rosary are scenes from the life of Jesus and Mary. By meditating on these sublime truths, we come to a better understanding of our religion: the Incarnation of the Lord, the Redemption, and the Christian life—present and future.

In the following outline the words in parentheses indicate practical applications to our daily lives.

The Joyful Mysteries

1. The messenger of God announces to Mary that she is to be the Mother of God. (Humility)
2. Mary visits and helps her cousin Elizabeth. (Love of Neighbor)
3. Mary gives birth to Jesus in a stable in Bethlehem. (Spirit of Poverty)
4. Jesus is presented in the Temple. (Obedience to God's Will)
5. Jesus is found in the Temple. (Fidelity to Vocation)

The Sorrowful Mysteries

1. Jesus undergoes his agony in the Garden of Gethsemane. (Spirit of Prayer)
2. Jesus is scourged at the pillar. (Modesty and Purity)
3. Jesus is crowned with thorns. (Courage)
4. Jesus carries the cross to Calvary. (Patience in Suffering)
5. Jesus dies on the cross for our sins. (Self-denial)

The Glorious Mysteries

1. Jesus rises from the dead. (Faith)
2. Jesus ascends into heaven. (Hope)
3. The Holy Spirit comes to the apostles and the Blessed Mother. (Wisdom, Love, Zeal, Fortitude)
4. The Mother of Jesus is taken into heaven. (Eternal Happiness)
5. Mary is crowned queen of heaven and earth. (Devotion to Mary and Final Perseverance)

20. Hail, Holy Queen

[963-975, 2617-2622, 2672-2675]

Hail, holy queen, mother of mercy, our life, our sweetness, and our hope. To you we cry, poor banished children of Eve; to you we send up our sighs, mourning and weeping in this valley of tears. Turn then, O most gracious advocate, your eyes of mercy toward us, and after this our exile, show unto us the blessed fruit of your womb, Jesus. O clement, O loving, O sweet virgin Mary.

Pray for us, O holy Mother of God.

Response: That we may be made worthy of the promises of Christ.

Let us pray: O God, whose only begotten Son, by his life, death, and resurrection, has purchased for us the rewards of eternal life, grant, we beseech you, that meditating upon these mysteries of the most holy rosary of the Blessed Virgin Mary, we may imitate what they contain and obtain what they promise. Through the same Christ our Lord. Amen.

21. Prayer to Our Redeemer
[1381]

Soul of Christ, sanctify me; body of Christ, save me.

Blood of Christ, inebriate me;

Water from the side of Christ, wash me.

Passion of Christ, strengthen me. O good Jesus, hear me. Within your wounds hide me. Never permit me to be separated from you. From the evil one protect me, at the hour of death call me, and bid me come to you that with your saints I may praise you forever. Amen.

22. Stations of the Cross
[617, 1674]
(Meditations on the Suffering and Death of Jesus)

Introductory Prayer
  1. Jesus is condemned to death on the cross.
  2. Jesus accepts his cross.
  3. Jesus falls the first time.
  4. Jesus meets his sorrowful Mother.
  5. Simon of Cyrene helps Jesus carry his cross.
  6. Veronica wipes the face of Jesus.
  7. Jesus falls the second time.
  8. Jesus meets and speaks to the women of Jerusalem.
  9. Jesus falls the third time.

10. Jesus is stripped of his garments.

11. Jesus is nailed to the cross.

12. Jesus dies on the cross.

13. Jesus is taken down from the cross.

14. Jesus is placed in the tomb.

Closing Prayer (recalling the Resurrection)

(At each station, contemplate the scene and pray a brief, heartfelt prayer.)

23. Prayer to Your Guardian Angel

[335, 336, 350-352]

Angel of God, my guardian dear, to whom his love commits me here, ever this day (night) be at my side, to light and guard, to rule and guide. Amen.

24. Prayer for the Faithful Departed

[958, 1032]

Eternal rest grant unto them, O Lord.

Response: And let perpetual light shine upon them.

May their souls and the souls of all the faithful departed, through the mercy of God, rest in peace.

Response: Amen.

25. Liturgical Prayers of the Mass

[1145-1162, 1345-1355]

Every Mass is an action not only of Christ but of the Church. As the central act of worship on the part of Catholics, it calls for community participation [1324-1326]. God speaks to you through his Revelation; you speak to him through your prayers, your songs, your responses [1157, 1158, 1356, 1357]. You offer yourselves and your gifts to him; he offers himself (through his priest) in an unbloody sacrifice. And, because the Mass is also a sacred banquet, you receive him as nourishment for the spirit [1382-1390].

For an explanation of the Mass, see pages 45 to 46 in this booklet. Recommended reading in this area is *What You Should Know About the*

Mass by Charlene Altemose, MSC. Order from Liguori Publications, Box 060, Liguori, MO 63057-9999. (Please enclose $3.95 plus $3.50 for postage and handling.)

To help you better understand the Mass and participate more fully, study the following order (or arrangement) of the Mass.

26. Order of the Mass (Community Prayer)

[1345-1355]

Introductory Rites
> Entrance Song
> Greeting
> Penitential Rite
> Gloria
> Opening Prayer

Liturgy of the Word

(We hear and respond to the Word of God.)
> First Reading
> Responsorial Psalm
> Second Reading
> Alleluia or Gospel Acclamation
> Gospel
> Homily
> Profession of Faith (Creed)
> General Intercessions (Prayer of the Faithful)

Liturgy of the Eucharist

(We offer Jesus to the Father.)
> Preparation and Offering of Gifts
> Prayer Over the Gifts
> Eucharistic Prayer
> (Our gifts of bread and wine become
>   the body and blood of Christ.)
> Memorial Acclamation

Lord's Prayer
Sign of Peace
Breaking of the Bread
Reception of Communion
Prayer After Communion
Concluding Rites
Blessing
Dismissal

27. A Method of Meditation (Private Prayer)

[2705-2708, 2723]

I. Preparation

As a remote preparation try to remain conscious of God as you go about your daily schedule. Frequently remind yourself of this truth: God is everywhere and is very interested in your welfare.

At the beginning of the meditation, make a deliberate Act of Faith regarding God's presence. Ask him for pardon of any faults. Ask for help to make a good meditation. Add a prayer to our Blessed Mother and other favorite saints for assistance.

II. Consideration

Read for a few minutes from the Bible or other spiritual book. Ask yourself *What have I read? What does it teach me? How have I acted in regard to this till now? What shall I do about it in the future?*

Since the advantage of meditation is not so much in the thinking as in the praying that it leads to, it is important to devote the greater part of meditation to affections (short prayers from the heart), petitions (requests for help from God), and resolutions (practical plans for changing your life, with God's help).

Affections: "Lord, I am sorry for having offended you." "Thank you for the blessings you have given me." "I want to love you above all things." "I praise you, Lord!" "Your will be done!" "I place my trust in you."

Petitions: Ask for whatever you need: for example, forgiveness of sins, greater confidence, help in a stressful situation, specific graces to forgive someone, to be more patient, to die a good death.

Resolutions: Make them short and specific, for example, to stop gossiping with…, to be kind to…, not to lose patience with…, to be faithful to times of prayer.

III. Conclusion

1. Thank God for the insights and graces gained during this meditation.
2. Repeat your resolutions.
3. Ask for help to keep your resolutions.
4. Choose some special thought or short prayer to carry with you during the day.

Further Suggestions for Meditative Prayer
[2709-2719, 2724]

1. Do not do all the talking yourself. Stop now and then to listen to the Lord. The inspirations he gives on occasion are wordless insights or sentiments that you "hear" in your heart.
2. Do not try to *feel* the acts of love and other affections you express. They are acts of your will and usually do not spill over into felt emotions. If you experience dissatisfaction because your mind keeps wandering, have patience with yourself. Enduring this inability to pray is a valuable part of your prayer.
3. If you are drawn at times to thinking about or looking silently at God— or you become vaguely aware of his presence—simply go along that way. But if you find your mind wandering, return to expressing affections such as love, praise, sorrow. Some people maintain this simple focus on God by slowly repeating a phrase—for example, "Lord Jesus Christ, have mercy on me"—or a single word such as "God" or "Jesus."

28. Benediction of the Most Blessed Sacrament
(Prayer to Christ in the Eucharist)
[1381]

As Catholics, it is our privilege to participate in offering the eucharistic sacrifice and in receiving holy Communion. But there are many additional acts of devotion that help extend Christ's real presence among us. Such a devotion is Benediction of the Most Blessed Sacrament.

Christ's promise is to be with us *always* (Matthew 28:20). The practice of reservation of the Blessed Sacrament arose early in the history of the Church. (This was for the convenience of the sick—that Communion might be taken to them.) People then began spontaneously to gather in the churches to pray and worship in the very presence of Christ. Later, because Christ's presence meant so much to them, they asked that the host be exhibited to them on a throne in a monstrance (an ornamental receptacle). Still later, prayers and songs were added, and the priest would bless the people with the host enthroned in the monstrance.

Benediction is an amazingly simple and beautifully proportioned act of worship. We begin by *contemplating* God's presence in our midst. (Most of the time we are so busy talking or doing things or going places that Christ hardly gets a chance to say anything to us. Contemplation means that we let God "soak into us.") Then follows the actual sacramental blessing: the priest makes the Sign of the Cross over us with the host enshrined in the monstrance. Finally, we make our spontaneous response in words of praise and thanksgiving.

While the congregation sings an opening song (any eucharistic hymn), the celebrant removes the host from the tabernacle, places it in a monstrance, and enthrones it on the altar. After he incenses the host (a symbolic action indicating our prayerful worship), a period of silent contemplation or public prayer ensues. Then, after the homily (if there is one), a hymn such as "Down in Adoration Falling" is sung.

The celebrant then says or sings a prayer such as the following:

Celebrant: Lord Jesus Christ, you gave us the Eucharist as the memorial of your suffering and death. May our worship of this sacrament of your body and blood help us to experience the salvation you won for us and the peace of the kingdom where you live with the Father and the Holy Spirit, one God, for ever and ever.

People: Amen.

The celebrant blesses the people with the host and then returns the Eucharist to the tabernacle. Afterward the people themselves may say or sing an acclamation such as the Divine Praises [2639-2643]:

> Blessed be God.
> Blessed be his holy name.
> Blessed be Jesus Christ, true God and true man.
> Blessed be the name of Jesus.
> Blessed be his most Sacred Heart.
> Blessed be his most Precious Blood.
> Blessed be Jesus in the most Holy Sacrament of the Altar.
> Blessed be the Holy Spirit, the Paraclete.
> Blessed be the great Mother of God, Mary most holy.
> Blessed be her holy and Immaculate Conception.
> Blessed be her glorious Assumption.
> Blessed be the name of Mary, Virgin and Mother.
> Blessed be Saint Joseph, her most chaste spouse.
> Blessed be God in his angels and in his saints.

LIVING THE FAITH IN THE SPIRIT OF VATICAN II

BY CHARLENE ALTEMOSE, MSC

Introductory Note

Our Catholic faith calls us to a way of life in imitation of Jesus and in accordance with Tradition and Church teachings. We assent by belief to truths our minds accept and fulfill certain commandments, but living the faith means more than that. This section contains practical ways Catholics carry out in daily life what the Church calls us to.

1. We Meet God in the Sacred Words of Scripture

[101-141]

Vatican II, stressing the importance of both the Old and New Testaments as God's revelation, encouraged Catholics to make the Bible an important part of their faith and spirituality [103, 104].

The Bible is more "user-friendly" for Catholics today for a variety of reasons. It's available in readable versions and convenient formats. Biblical scholarship has shed light on obscure passages, making the Bible more understandable. The discovery of ancient manuscripts has led to a greater knowledge of the culture, customs, geography, and peoples of biblical lands [119].

The liturgy provides a greater variety of Scripture readings in the language of the people. Religious education is now focusing on a "lectionary-based catechesis," instruction based on the liturgical readings. The increase in the number of study groups and adult-education programs in parishes throughout the country demonstrate the interest of today's Catholics in the Bible [131-133].

The Nature of the Bible
[101-112]

Although the Bible comes to us in the guise of a printed book, more accurately it is the record of God's relationship with his people and their responses. This living experience is seen through the eyes of certain individuals who recorded the events under the inspiration of the Holy Spirit. The Bible deals with what any relationship demands: discoveries, difficulties, conversion, change, and love.

In the Bible we meet people like ourselves who love, hate, backslide, sin, dream, and despair. They are prototypes of how God loves humans through any situation and of how humans relate to God in a variety of ways. Though time and culture differ, we can get caught up in the biblical drama and identify with the persons we meet within the sacred pages [105-108].

The Bible is not a frozen collection of tales of the past; rather, it is the Lord speaking to us today. The Bible is a useful avenue to strengthen our love-relationship with the Lord [101-104].

Catholics believe the Bible is the inspired Word of God written in the words of human authors who, under the inspiration of the Holy Spirit, selected a literary form, style, and genre that effectively conveyed the experience of the Lord. These ancient writers were more concerned with the meanings of events than with exact details: the *why* rather than the *what* [109-112].

The Challenge of Fundamentalism
[115-119]

Although Catholics consider the Bible part of the living Tradition, some Christians consider the Bible to be the only source of faith. For them, all the fundamental truths are contained within the Scriptures, hence the label *fundamentalist*. Fundamentalists often challenge, and in their zeal attempt to change, the faith of those whose beliefs differ from theirs [108].

Fundamentalists believe that the exact words of the Bible have been dictated by God, that the Bible is the only way God has revealed himself, and that all doctrine is found in Scripture and can be proven there. Without considering the literary forms used by the authors of the Scriptures, fundamentalists take the Bible literally and refuse to consider the human role in the compiling of Scripture [110].

How can you deal with overzealous fundamentalists?

First, be confident and familiar with your own faith so you will not feel threatened by other interpretations. Second, listen courteously to what fundamentalists say without becoming defensive. Finally, ask them about their own faith commitment. In this way, you redirect their attention and focus them on their faith rather than on yours.

A response such as "I understand what you are saying, but I don't see it that way" is amicably assertive, yet preserves your right to your own viewpoint. If the person persists in his or her opinion, be friendly yet firm. Don't attempt to counter the fundamentalist's Bible quotes with your own. Catholics can well imitate and admire the zeal of fundamentalist friends but not their methods or opinions.

The Bible as Ideal Spiritual Enrichment
[131-133]

Reading the Bible is a powerful way to experience the presence of the Lord in your life. The Bible is the Living Word, and God continues to reveal himself today through the Scriptures. The following guidelines can aid Catholics in utilizing the Scriptures in a more meaningful way.

- Make a conscious effort to listen actively and attentively to the Scripture readings during the Liturgy of the Word. This not only enhances your appreciation of the Scriptures but also contributes toward a deeper spirituality and a more meaningful liturgy.
- Set aside some time each day for reflective reading of the Bible. Consider it as necessary spiritual nourishment and enrichment. Use a

Bible you are comfortable marking up and underlining. Begin and end your Scripture reading with a prayer. In order to understand obscure passages better, take time to read the introduction to the biblical book from which you are reading. Who wrote it? Why was it written? What were the cultural and religious customs of the time in which the book was written?

- Select passages you can relate to and listen to what God tells you. Imagine the scene, the setting, and the people involved. Use all your senses: seeing, feeling, hearing, touch, and smell. Put yourself in the picture. Ask yourself *What does this passage mean for me now in my situation? What does this passage teach me to believe? What is it helping me to become? How is it improving my relationship with God and with others?* Either converse familiarly with the Lord or just listen and relax in his caring presence. Perhaps just one sentence "jumps out" at you. If so, stay with that inspiration; it will be enough.
- Share the Scriptures with others. Join a Bible-study group led by someone with a Scripture background and the expertise to explain unclear passages. Be aware that the Bible says different things to different people and that practical applications vary.

The Bible is dynamic. On every page God breaks into our lives in mysterious ways.

Prayer Before Reading the Bible
[131-133]

Our Father, who art in heaven, sacred is your Word. Your kingdom come, your words be heard on earth as they are in heaven. Give us today your sacred Word. Forgive our neglect of it in the past as we forgive those who neglect us. Lead us toward an encounter with you each time we delve into the Scriptures. For your presence, your power, and your glory are ever present among us now and forever. Amen.

Prayer After Reading the Bible

Lord, I thank you for your special presence to me during this time. I thank you for the opportunity to know you and your ways better. Open my heart that I put into practice that which you have revealed to me. Thank you, Lord, for the gift and love of your sacred Word. Amen.

2. We Worship the Lord in Liturgy and Sacrament
[1136-1209, 1322-1419]

Liturgy
[1136-1209]

The liturgical community gathering known as the Mass is the soul of Catholic worship. We consider here the external changes, attitudes, and practical ways for making Mass a meaningful celebration [1324-1327].

Our coming together in worship as a people and a community is called *Mass* because we are sent out in "mission" to spread the Good News. The Mass is also referred to as *liturgy, the worship of the people*, or *Eucharist*, which means "thanksgiving." Throughout the ages, the Mass changed from a simple community gathering to a ritualized formal worship service conducted solely by the priest. To bridge the gap between priest and people and to promote greater laity participation, Vatican II initiated changes, variety, and options in the eucharistic worship [1328-1333].

The altar of sacrifice, the focal point of worship, is placed so the priest faces the people [1182, 1383]. The language of the people replaces Latin. The laity serve in various liturgical capacities: lectors read the Scriptures, commentators make announcements and offer petitions, eucharistic ministers distribute Communion, cantors lead the congregation in song. Others bring the gifts in procession. The congregation also joins in with responses and song. Although the presider and the assisting ministers set the tone, all who take part are responsible for fitting worship [903, 1143]. The following observations can contribute toward making the liturgy a rich faith experience on both the personal and communal level.

Practical Guidelines for Participation at Liturgy
[1345-1355]

The Mass is an opportunity to worship and honor God. Along with the priest, we are offering the most precious gift we can, the Lord himself. While waiting for the Mass to begin, we can offer to the Lord the concerns of all who worship with us. In this way, we make the Mass a true community celebration. We pray and sing together, and we observe silence in common. (Private devotions, as their name indicates, are out of place in the public ceremony called the Mass.)

We should listen to the Scriptures attentively; the Lord is speaking to us. We recite the Creed as a renewal of our baptism commitment. We offer ourselves and our gifts to the Lord and join in acclaiming the sacramental presence of Christ and the Father. We should extend ourselves in true reconciliation to those around us at the sign of peace. We believe with all our hearts that the Lord truly heals: "Only say the word, and I shall be healed." As we receive Communion, our wholehearted "Amen" says, "Yes, Lord, I believe in you; make me a better person." The liturgy brings the sacramental presence of Christ into our midst. The final blessing, "Go in peace, to love and serve the Lord," sends us forth to continue the mission of Christ.

The more active and attentive we are at Mass, the greater will be the intensity of Christ's presence in the world. No matter how solemn or simple, the eucharistic liturgy is God's perfect gift to us. It is our frail imperfect human attempt to "Do this in remembrance…" and to celebrate in ritual and symbol the divine mystery of Christ's sacramental presence.

Sacraments
[1113-1134, 1210-1666]

In the seven sacraments, we celebrate through ritual and symbol the Lord's special presence in individual lives. The sacramental life of the Church is an integral part of our Catholic faith [1076].

The sacraments are moments of God touching our lives in a special way and opportunities for growth in our relationship with God [1533]. The sacraments of initiation—baptism, confirmation, and Eucharist— are moments of new beginnings, recommitment, and continued spiritual strength [1212]. Moments of healing are experienced in reconciliation, or the sacrament of penance, and anointing of the sick [1420, 1421]. Vocational commitments are sacramentally celebrated through matrimony and holy orders [1534, 1535].

The sacramental life calls us to continual conversion. We are always on the way toward greater union with God. Through the sacraments, we respond to the Lord's desire to be with us always and especially at significant moments of our journey of faith [1123].

Sacraments are neither isolated actions nor magical moments. They are the continuing presence of Christ in the world. The more intense our sacramental life, the greater is our Christian witness. Liturgy and life are closely bonded [1124].

Over the years the true nature of some of the sacraments became clouded by undue emphasis on supplementary rituals or unbalanced theology. The Second Vatican Council called for revision of the sacramental rites so their original purpose and essence would be more obvious [1125, 1126].

Sacraments of Initiation. In the early Church, baptism, confirmation, and Eucharist were considered as one ritual when new members came into the Church [1212]. When infant baptism became common in the Western Church, the sacraments of initiation became three separate rites but remained as one ceremony in the Eastern rites [1252]. Vatican II revised the Rite of the Sacraments of Initiation so the baptism-confirmation-Eucharist link is reestablished. This change is most evident when adults who have gone through the RCIA become Catholics and receive the sacraments of initiation at the Easter Vigil [1247-1249].

Baptism. Although the Church has practiced infant baptism for centuries, Vatican II shifted the theological stance of the sacrament. The Rite of Baptism for Children now being used emphasizes the role of the parents [1250-1252]. When a child is baptized, the parents hand on a tradition and legacy they value. Before an infant is brought to baptism, the Church requires that the parents be suitably catechized, be active Catholics, and be instructed in the meaning of baptism and their responsibility as their child's primary religious educators [2226, 2252, 2253].

Confirmation. After confirmation became a separate rite, it was customary to consider it a sacrament of maturity. It began to be received later, usually in the early teens. Currently, practices vary, especially regarding the age when confirmation is given, since confirmation is governed by diocesan norms [1307, 1308, 1318].

Penance (Reconciliation). The new Rite of Reconciliation stresses the healing presence of Christ. No longer is it merely the telling of specific sins but a compassionate forgiveness of one's sinfulness in an attitude of sorrow. Penitents can opt to receive the sacrament either anonymously in the confessional or face to face in a reconciliation room [1441, 1442].

Anointing of the Sick. Anointing of the sick gives spiritual strength and healing to those who are aged or ill. It is no longer "extreme unction," given only to those in danger of death. It can be received any time during illness. Parishes conduct communal anointings to show a compassionate solidarity with the sick and to experience and celebrate corporately the healing presence of Christ [1499-1532].

Holy Orders. The *Decree on the Ministry and Life of Priests* recognizes that "the pastoral and human circumstances of the priest have been thoroughly changed." As leader of the community of faith, the priest is responsible for implementing the reforms of Vatican II at the local level. This demands modifying styles of leadership, working in collaboration with laity, updating and adjusting to newer modes. The priest does the work of Christ and in his ministry mirrors Christ's compassionate and healing qualities [1562-1566].

3. We Serve the Lord in Ministry
[897-913]

The Catholic faith lives on today because in every age persons faithful to their baptismal commitment heeded the call, "As each one has received a gift, use it to serve one another as good stewards of God's varied grace" (1 Peter 4:10). Christ's ministry was carried forward; the Church grew.

The Second Vatican Council provided direction and opened new channels for Catholics to serve in a variety of ministries in the Church.

When we think of ministry, we usually think of what we do and how we serve. But unlike other works or jobs, "ministry in service to the Church" is a response to a special call. There is present a deeper reality, a sacred dimension that is Trinitarian: creative, redemptive, and sanctifying.

Creative. God the Father in creation extended himself most generously, diffusing his presence with his infinite love. He thereby gifted all creation with his infinite goodness. We are called to share our giftedness, extending ourselves in love to others, rechanneling the talents we've been given and using them for the benefit of others and the growth of the kingdom of God [279-324].

Redemptive. Jesus as God and man perfectly fused the dichotomies of divine and human in his person. He responded to all human needs and ultimately to the need for redemption. He modeled his ministry on the team approach, depending on and working with others. Redemptive ministry responds to the needs of all. It is men and women, clergy and laity, old and young, rich and poor, working, praying, and celebrating together, sharing a common goal: building up the Body of Christ [456-460, 535-560].

Sanctifying. The Holy Spirit vitalizes and energizes the Church, providing spiritual impetus and growth. Through the Spirit's abiding presence, ministries are endowed with a deeper reality, an attitude that enlivens. The role of the Spirit is vital because the elements of a caring presence and compassion are essential for any ministry [683-688].

Here are some practical ways these spiritual qualities can be applied on the parish level toward more effective ministry.

Before Vatican II, priests were solely responsible for the parish. Today the viability of the Church is also the responsibility of the people. Needs vary from place to place and from parish to parish. The degree of lay involvement also fluctuates, depending on the availability of priests, their willingness to allow the laity to participate more fully, and the initiative and cooperation of the people. Parish councils, mandatory in some dioceses, advise the pastor in the administration of the parish [911].

Lay leadership is to be encouraged and supported. It is the task of every parish to assess its needs and organize meaningful ministries accordingly. The variety of ministries is as varied as are human needs. Wherever there are cries for support and compassion, wherever there are hurts in need of healing, there is ministry. Parish ministries are generally grouped under the following areas: sacramental, educational, administrative, pastoral ministry, and outreach [898-913].

Although the purpose of ministry never changes, the ways Christ's mission is fulfilled changes with the times. New techniques, attitudes, tools, and skills are necessary for productive and effective ministry in the Church today.

Permanent Diaconate
[1569-1571, 1596]

One of the significant ways Catholic men can participate more directly in ministry is through the diaconate. Deacons played an important role in the early Church. As time passed, however, the need for them diminished, and the diaconate was inactive for many centuries. Vatican II, seeing its value for today's Church, reactivated the permanent diaconate.

After a period of formation, married or celibate men can be ordained deacons and receive holy orders. However, the permanent diaconate is a ministry in its own right and is not the preparatory step to priesthood, as is the transitional diaconate. A permanent deacon is assigned by the bishop to liturgical and service roles in parishes or diocesan institutions. He can assist at liturgies, baptize, give homilies, and preside at other services, either full time or along with his regular occupation. He is also a valuable asset in marriage preparation and counseling.

Through their service in administrative, liturgical, educational, and pastoral roles, deacons provide a vital ministry, especially in areas where there is a shortage of priests and a need for lay leadership. The role of the deacon is expected to become more prominent and prevalent in the Church of the future.

Role of Women
[369-373, 791, 814, 1934-1938]

Throughout the history of the Church, women have always served and ministered. The gospels and the Acts of the Apostles record specific instances of women's influence and presence. Prior to Vatican II, women, mainly religious, were directly involved in ministry in schools, hospitals, parishes, orphanages, and other Church-sponsored institutions.

Women's role in the Church was specifically addressed in the Vatican II *Decree on the Apostolate of Lay People:* "Since in our days women are taking an increasingly active share in the whole life of society, it is very important that their participation in the various sectors of the Church's apostolate should likewise develop" (9).

Although women's participation in some areas needs fuller recognition, in the past twenty-five years women have become more actively involved in ministry and pastoral service. Women are becoming increasingly visible in liturgical celebrations as readers, eucharistic ministers, and leaders of music.

Women have always been in the forefront of education in the Church. As more women enroll in advanced degree programs in theology and pastoral ministry, they can expect to move into leadership roles in greater numbers. More laywomen serve in academic positions in colleges and seminaries, as directors of religious education (DREs), and catechists. They serve as directors of diocesan offices, vicars for religious, bishops' assistants, canon lawyers, tribunal members, and in other diocesan administrative positions.

In areas where there are few priests or where priests are available only for periodic liturgies, women are administering parishes so that a stable presence of Church is available. Women serve as pastoral ministers, counselors, hospital chaplains, spiritual directors, and in other ministries not generally open to the laity before Vatican II.

As ministry needs expand and women become more aware of opportunities to share their gifts, we can expect to see women's leadership roles in Church ministry increase even more in the future.

4. We Live Our Faith Through Life Commitments
[1877]

Catholicism is lived in its fullness when the faith we profess in worship is carried into daily life and activities. Our lives, our families, our faith through baptism, are among God's gifts to us. In addition, God gives us a free will, so we can make our own choices and decisions [1730-1748].

Life Commitment and Vocation
[2004]

One of the most responsible choices we have is the state of life we will follow. Our life commitment mirrors our covenant relationship with God, for through our individual lives and vocations, we serve the Lord. Saint Paul exhorts: "Live in a manner worthy of the call you have received, with all humility and gentleness…" (Ephesians 4:1).

Our decision to live in a specific state of life does not lessen our responsibility to live a faith-filled life. It merely channels our actions into areas where we can use our gifts and the opportunities that come our way. Regardless of the life commitment we have chosen, we are responsible for contributing to the good of the world. Vatican II reminds us of our common call to holiness: "All Christians in any state or walk of life are called to the fullness of Christian life and to the perfection of love, and by this holiness a more human manner of life is fostered also in earthly society" (*The Church,* 40) [828, 1426, 2013, 2028].

We are all called by virtue of our baptismal vows to live life faithfully and to let our light shine before all. We have the light; what are we doing with it [1267-1270]?

Role of the Laity in the Workplace
[897-913]

The call to holiness extends beyond our private life commitment and Church allegiance into all spheres of daily activity. Religion fully lived is an around-the-clock endeavor, an in-the-workplace task. [1878-1885]

In the aftermath of their increased participation in ministry, the basic role of the laity cannot be overlooked: "They [the laity] live in the world, that is, they are engaged in each and every work and business of the earth and in the ordinary circumstances of social and family life, which, as it were, constitute their very existence. There they are called by God that, being led by the spirit of the Gospel, they may contribute to the sanctification of the world…" (*The Church,* 31). Therefore, the laity's task is to inspire a basic goodness, flavoring the world with the salt of Christian values and the leaven of holiness [1905-1912].

We Catholics gather at Sunday worship to revitalize and energize our faith, and we scatter on Monday to our workplaces. It is in this "animating the temporal affairs from within" that the liturgy is brought to its fruitful completion [1166, 1167].

Gospel values can be instilled into the sin-scarred, evil-infested world by those who work in its midst. The kingdom of God is brought to earth in homes, offices, schools, stores, businesses, and hospitals. Everywhere there are people, there is work. And where there is work, there is the Church. Catholics need to take along into the workplace a priority of values, coloring every activity in the world of daily work with inspiring goodness and truth.

Married State
[1601-1666]

Throughout the ages, the love between man and woman has been extolled as sacred and celebrated in solemn rituals. Those entering marriage make a commitment not only to each other but also to God, so the Church raised marriage to the dignity of a sacrament. Through lives of mutual love, the married attain holiness and witness to Christ's love for the Church [1601].

One of the main responsibilities of married couples is to provide an atmosphere of goodness in the home. They are also bound to raise their children with Christian values. Formerly, parents relied almost solely on professional religious for their children's religious formation. Today the parents are the prime religious educators and play an active role in their children's sacramental preparation [902, 1653-1658, 2204-2206].

It has been proven that no matter how much outside instruction children receive, it will avail nothing if values are not carried out in the home. The nurturing of the children in the faith is one of the most serious responsibilities parents have. Parents are to live their commitment responsibly, that is, according to a formed and informed conscience [2221-2231].

89

The number of children a married couple decides upon is a personal decision. However, their method of family planning must be in accord with Church teachings [1652]. The Church stands firm in its upholding of the sacredness of life at all stages [2259-2283].

In the past the ministry of the Church has been oriented toward the traditional family of mother, father, and children. Today, we must recognize and embrace other, nontraditional situations. The Church needs to extend pastoral care toward those couples who, for whatever reason, remain childless. Many single parents are trying to raise their children alone. Sensitive pastoral concern must be extended when the "ideal" family is often extolled and the childless couple or single parent may feel uneasy. No matter what their circumstances, those in the married state and the parental role live out their commitment insofar as they attempt to make a Christ-centered, value-oriented home [2201-2206].

The marriage commitment has undergone many challenges in recent years. In an attempt to alleviate the failure of marriages because of incompatibility or immaturity, Vatican II has authorized the establishment of comprehensive marriage preparation programs [1632].

Separated and Divorced
[1650, 2382-2386]

After a couple separates, a civil divorce is often required for legal purposes. This civil divorce in itself does not constitute an impediment to the sacraments for the Catholic party.

If, after much investigation and discussion, it is proven that the parties were not maturely or morally responsible and a true marriage bond never existed, an *annulment* is granted. An annulment is not a divorce.

Many factors contribute to the increased divorce rate: our mobile society, loosened family ties, the pressures of modern living. The Church realizes that divorce affects many Catholics and has increased its concern for ministry to the divorced and separated. Most dioceses have established pastoral care and ministry for the separated and divorced.

Although society's attitude toward divorce has changed, the trauma of divorce is a major stressor. It is a deeply rooted personal crisis that affects those who experience it at the depths of their being. The Church is called upon to be caring and concerned to these people. The greatest empowerment and most effective healing happens when the divorced minister to others who are divorced. Those who have walked in the same moccasins are able to empathize more. In many areas, there are support groups of divorced persons ministering to one another.

The Church needs to extend pastoral care to the divorced and to accept them into the faith community. By their trauma and pain, the divorced and separated remain a potent sign that the suffering Church needs to experience Christ's compassion, healing, and understanding. (For fuller discussion on separation and divorce read *With Open Arms: Catholics, Divorce and Remarriage*, Liguori Publications.)

Single State
[2004, 2348, 2349]

Although most people marry, many live their commitment as single persons by choice or by circumstance. Though the Catholic Church is becoming more aware of its responsibility to minister to singles, there is still much that can be done toward making the singles feel fully accepted. The Church needs to recognize more clearly the validity of the single life in the world as a call no less sacred than the call to be married, to be ordained, or to be a religious. The Church also needs to be sensitive in its overall planning of programs and parish celebrations. They should be all-inclusive so members of the faith community, no matter what their state of life, can take part without embarrassment or without feeling out of place.

Widowed State
[2349]

One of the first ministries of the early Christians was the care of the widowed. The need today is no less real. In fact, because of increased longevity and other social conditions, there is an increase in the number of widows and widowers.

Each parish and neighborhood has its share of those who have lost their mates. The Church needs to be aware of their presence and provide ways for them to attain meaning in their lives. The parish may have a formal program, but caring compassion and a human presence to walk with the widowed in their grief is an even more effective way to carry out the Church's call to care for all its members [2443].

5. We Respond in Faith to Social Needs

[1928-1948]

Our responsibility in life is not just to become better persons. As John Donne wrote, "No man is an island." Because the kingdom of God is a kingdom of justice, love, and peace, the Church's mission includes responsibility for the humanization of the world in the fullest sense. As Catholics, we need to be concerned about actively striving to bring into the world Christ's justice and peace. Our Christian commitment calls us to "Christify" the world, to make the love of Christ more visible and more fully experienced. To be true to our moral responsibility, we are called to develop a sincere social consciousness. Morality consists in more than mere avoidance of acts that are "sins." We must strive to squelch the sinfulness in ourselves and in the world around us [1877-1879].

A mere awareness of the presence of evils in our midst is insufficient. Saint James warns: "If a brother or sister has nothing to wear and has no food for the day, and one of you says to them, 'Go in peace, keep warm, and eat well,' but you do not give them the necessities of the body, what good is it? So also faith of itself, if it does not have works, is dead" (James 2:15-17). A living faith requires active concern for the oppressed, the homeless, and the downtrodden [2443-2448].

Social concerns must embrace our untiring efforts to eliminate hunger, disease, discrimination, poverty, and war on all levels. We are called to become actively involved and to strive toward solidarity with those who suffer, those who need healing, those with whom we can share our abundance. We must link ourselves directly with the poor [1913-1917].

The activities of everyday life mirror the creative work of God and share in the redemptive act of saving the world. The corporal works of mercy are not merely charitable deeds under the auspices of pious organizations. Rather, the corporal works are carried out in the daily grind of our lives. Farmers, butchers, and grocers feed the hungry; water purification crews and waiters give drink to the thirsty; morticians and coroners bury the dead; parole officers, guards, counselors, and fellow inmates tend the imprisoned; construction workers, carpenters, plumbers, and electricians do their part in sheltering the homeless; seamstresses, tailors, and shopkeepers clothe the naked. But we are challenged to do more; we are challenged to extend ourselves beyond our own concerns [2447].

All of us are called to permeate the structures of society with so much goodness that it oozes out and counters evil. If a bad apple affects the good ones, cannot we as Christians and Catholics reverse the procedure and be the good that affects the bad?

The responsibility for infusing values into secular society resides primarily with the laity, who can influence laws, social structures, and the civic community with a Christian sense of life. It is a challenging task in a world where materialism and standards of success run counter to basic Christian values [1929-1933].

The challenge of the Christian is to be countercultural, to go against the false promises of the world and to fight evil and sinfulness with saintliness and goodness. Without this renewal and perfecting of the social order, the building up of the Body of Christ cannot be effected, for it occurs in the world by a serious concern for the common good [1905-1917, 1939-1942].

Today we face social concerns previously unheard of. Modern medicine can do marvels, but we take a stand about genetic tampering, the right to life, and life-support systems that interfere with natural laws [2292-2295].

The abortion issue touches every aspect of life. Its profound moral implications plague the nation's lawmakers, the medical profession, the educational system, and the very foundation of society, the family [2270-2275]. The Church continues to affirm and uphold the sacredness of life at every stage of development. Catholics must not only abide by natural and God-given laws but also take an active stance in moral issues revolving around the sacredness of all life [2258-2283, 2319, 2322].

Our social consciousness must also extend toward preserving the earth. "Increase and multiply and preserve the earth" is the Genesis mandate [307, 373, 2427]. In our day this includes working toward a healthier, safer environment by avoiding pollution and littering, recycling, and using wisely our natural resources without wastefulness. Environmental concerns are an essential part of a Christian's social justice agenda [2402, 2415, 2456].

Concern for goodness reaches beyond our own nation into the global community to espouse justice and lasting peace for all peoples. Our concern for justice cannot be displayed in violent ways. True to the beatitudes, we must hunger and thirst for justice, yet in a nonviolent way, which in essence is the way of Christ. Our social structures and lifestyles must be vitalized by the spirit of nonviolence [1938-1942, 2302-2306].

Nonviolence creates an atmosphere of true liberty, where everyone can live peaceably and partake of the goods of the earth. To assist our sisters and brothers to reach their full potential as God intended, and to do so in a Christian manner, involves striving for peace within ourselves and within our relationships. Peace and justice in the world will come about only if we ease suffering, not inflict it. A deep Christian concern encourages those systems of justice that aim to save humanity from its own selfishness [2302-2317].

A fully formed social conscience likewise does all in its power to support those organizations that work toward the betterment of the human condition. It is informed and actively involved in social and political issues that affect the common good on local, national, and global levels [1905-1912].

In *Building the Earth,* Teilhard de Chardin challenges: "What we need is a passionate love of growth and of being. Life is moving toward unification. Our hope will become a reality only if it's expressed in greater cohesion and human solidarity. The future is in our hands. How shall we decide" [1939-1942, 1948]?

In his closing address at the Second Vatican Council, Pope Paul VI noted that "the story of the Good Samaritan is the model of the spirituality of the Church today." Renewal makes no sense unless the Church aims at serving wounded humanity and healing life's hurts. The ultimate norm of an authentic Catholic lies in the response to the query "How caring and compassionate am I" [2083, 2443, 2822]?

6. We Share and Spread the Good News

There are many different ways to spread the gospel. The practice of evangelization and the proper use of the RCIA are two examples.

Evangelization
[904-913]

Our basic baptismal commitment calls us to make the kingdom of God more visible on earth. Evangelization calls us to continue Christ's mission: "Go, therefore, and make disciples of all nations, baptizing them..." (Matthew 28:19) [849, 1257].

Although evangelization is a recurrent theme in the gospels, the word has now taken on nuances comparatively new to Catholic thinking. To avoid confusion it may be helpful to begin by pointing out what evangelization is *not*. It does not mean using outright conversion tactics such as foisting beliefs on new members. It does not mean trying to persuade persons who already have a religious commitment to accept the Catholic faith. The vision of evangelization is broader than merely the effort to draw others into the Faith [850, 851].

In his encyclical on evangelization, Pope Paul VI notes: "The Church evangelizes when, in seeking to convert, she relies solely on the power of the message she proclaims." To evangelize, in essence, is to proclaim the Good News and to be a more visible sign of God's presence in the world. At the heart of evangelization is an inner change, which affects all life's values. External works flow from the inner attitudes [2044-2047].

The tasks of evangelization are sharing the Good News with those who have never heard it, the spiritual renewal of the baptized, and the promotion of unity among Christians [821, 905].

The baptized are called to evangelize as well as to be evangelized by actively proclaiming the gospel and living it faithfully and fully [901-913].

How do Catholics evangelize? They do it by living in such a way that no matter what they do, where they are, or whom they reach, they diffuse goodness into the world. Each time Catholics witness to God's love and better the human condition, they are evangelizing. Catholics embody the message of Christ and proclaim the Good News with their lives. Evangelization is not limited to the formal ministries of catechizing, teaching, and serving in the Church [5-7, 910, 911].

You can be an effective evangelizer without even realizing it simply by example and presence. This is true of the sick and infirm who witness to the suffering Christ by nobly accepting their plight. Evangelization succeeds primarily by example and motivation rather than direct confrontation. Others find the Catholic way of life attractive and are drawn to inquire about it.

It is appropriate at times to evangelize actively by taking the initiative. Reach out to inactive Catholics, inviting them to return. Share your faith with those you sense are searching and questioning [4-10].

In order to do this, you need to feel comfortable with your own beliefs and to be conversant about your faith. Most Catholics today are aware that a religious education that ended with grade school or high school is insufficient in postconciliar times. Through continuing education programs and Catholic reading, you can keep informed of the ways Catholics today can understand the faith and proclaim the Good News more effectively [5-7].

Evangelization is "building up the Body of Christ" by positive means; it is inviting others to follow Christ by an innate magnetic attractiveness and witness to the gospel [2472].

RCIA—Rite of Christian Initiation of Adults
[1232, 1233, 1247-1249, 1285]

One of the most significant ways Catholics today can be evangelizers is to become involved in the Rite of Christian Initiation of Adults (RCIA). Since 1988 the RCIA has been mandated as the ordinary way adults are brought into full communion with the Catholic faith, whether from another Christian denomination or through baptism. The RCIA is designed to be a progressive journey of faith and a recurrent experience of conversion not only for the searcher but also for the whole Catholic community of faith.

The formation of new members is a communal responsibility. It encompasses each phase of parish life: witnessing, praying together, studying Scripture, sharing liturgy, and fellowship. The RCIA is not a parish program nor something to study about. The RCIA is a parish's call to conversion; it is evangelization in action at the local level.

Although the primary aim of the RCIA is the formation of new Catholics, a parish in which the RCIA flourishes experiences additional benefits. These include improved liturgies, greater community spirit and parish pride, and more active involvement and participation in parish activities and celebrations. There also will be an increased interest in adult education and formation.

Catholics within the parish become involved in the RCIA by being sponsors, working on the RCIA team, sharing personal faith stories, and actively searching out those who have no faith community or identity.

The RCIA is a gradual process that embodies the elements of a growing relationship. Through four specific phases, the inquirers move from casual acquaintance to full commitment [1229-1232].

Period of Evangelization and Precatechumenate. This is the time of getting acquainted. Those contemplating the Catholic faith—called inquirers—join with Catholics in informal discussions, ask questions, get rid of stereotyped ideas, undo fears or anxieties, and share their personal faith stories.

Period of Catechumenate. After the inquirers have decided to become Catholic, the Rite of Acceptance Into the Order of Catechumens is celebrated. During this time, the catechumens enter more deeply into the formation in faith. This period may last from several months to several years. Catechumens attend the Liturgy of the Word and participate more fully in the Church's liturgical life. They receive a sponsor who walks the journey of faith with them in a one-on-one relationship in which they feel free to ask questions and share their faith journey.

Period of Purification and Enlightenment. This stage of deeper commitment ordinarily begins on the First Sunday of Lent and is celebrated in a solemn rite at the cathedral of the diocese. The catechumens write their names in the book of the elect. The Lenten liturgies center on forgiveness, and the elect express their readiness through the scrutinies. The catechumens' example serves as a reminder of our constant need for purification and spiritual renewal [1438].

The climax of the catechumenate, the most solemn celebration of the Church year, takes place at the Easter Vigil on Holy Saturday evening. The sacraments of initiation—baptism, confirmation, Eucharist—are bestowed, and the new, full-fledged Catholics are now called neophytes [1212, 1233].

Period of Mystagogy. A post-Easter period of continued instruction and formation integrates the neophyte more fully into the community of faith. *Mystagogia* is a Greek word meaning "being initiated into mystery." The new Catholics are introduced into a greater explanation of the faith and of the various ministries in the parish [1075, 1233].

The Influence of the RCIA
[1886-1896]

The new Catholics' energy and enthusiasm for the Faith can be a catalyst for lifelong Catholics to become more involved. In its gradual unfolding, the RCIA process calls to mind the challenge and responsibility of every Catholic. The spiritual growth and maturity of a parish community can be measured in part by its understanding of the basic RCIA rationale.

The RCIA brings to parishioners a deeper sense of what conversion means and emphasizes the Church's identity as a community of faith and the people of God. When carried out ideally as intended, the RCIA becomes a most powerful sign of a Church alive and of a community of faith that understands its mission to bring the reign of Christ more intensely into the world.

The RCIA, then, can be the most effective avenue for evangelization on the local level.

7. We Respect Other Religions

[816,830]

In our age of increased global awareness, cultural mingling, and media coverage, religious pluralism is an obvious fact.Vatican II recognized the vast array of religious expressions in the world and addressed the issue in its *Declaration on the Relation of the Church to Non-Christian Religions:* "Men look to their different religions for an answer to the unsolved riddles of human existence....The Catholic Church rejects nothing of what is true and holy in these religions" (1-2) [842-843].

Catholics are to respect, preserve, and promote the spiritual and moral good found in all religions as well as the values in their society and culture [2104].

Special mention is made of our indebtedness to the Jewish faith. The Old Testament is the basis and root of Christianity. Jesus was a practicing Jew, and many Christian rituals stem from Jewish customs and traditions [574-594].

Although other religions have risen out of the human quest for God, Christianity is God becoming human. The Council presented a dynamic concept of "Church" as a divine mystery, but it upheld the conviction that the full revelation of God through Jesus is embodied in the teachings and Traditions of the Catholic Church under the direction of the pope. It recognizes, too, that other Christian bodies, as the "Church of Christ," contain certain aspects of the faith: "Many elements of sanctification and of truth are found outside its visible confines [of the Catholic Church]" (*The Church,* 8) [816, 819, 830, 855, 856].

Practical Guidelines Toward Interfaith Understanding

[821, 855, 856]

The *Decree on Ecumenism* further bridged the gap between religions and set forth useful guidelines for fruitful dialogue.

• Have a clear understanding of and be conversant with your own faith. Those who worship differently are sincere in their attempt to communicate with the Divine in ways they perceive and believe [847, 2106].

• Be willing to interpret another's faith in its best light, giving it the benefit of a good interpretation. Keep an openness and suspend judgment about the motives of other belief systems. Try to see the value in others' beliefs, focusing on what is held in common rather than what divides [1636].

• Develop a deep respect for the variety of ways in which others experience the Divine in their lives, realizing that people's basic religious view results from culture and heritage [855, 856].

Catholics today have many opportunities for interfaith understanding and dialogue. The climate of openness allows greater freedom than formerly for Catholics to discuss their religious beliefs with others and learn how others approach God [1636].

It is useful to heed the advice of Mahatma Gandhi: "I open my doors and windows allowing all cultures and religions to blow about freely, but I refuse to be swept off my feet by any."

The call to religious openness is basic if we are to live peaceably and in harmony with all peoples. Father Avery Dulles, S.J., summed up the ecumenical spirit in an address on Church unity: "To be truly Catholic, in the literal sense of the word, is to be universal and open to all truth and goodness from whatever source it may come" [849-856].

A Guide to Action for Today's Catholic

Today's Catholic, in keeping with the spirit of Vatican II,

• realizes that Jesus is the key and focal point of human destiny and that our call is to continue his mission
• strives to become a fully integrated human being by working for moral goodness in his or her personal and work life and in relationship to God and to others
• is faithful to his or her baptismal commitment by being active in a community of faith, participating regularly in the sacraments, and acknowledging the tenets of faith expressed in the Creed
• develops an intense personal relationship with God through Jesus by a deep life of prayer and love of the Bible
• recognizes the presence of Jesus as personified in the pope, bishops, pastors, and people of God

- lives fully in the spirit of "How much good *can* I do?" not minimally in a "What *must* I do?" attitude
- contributes to the betterment of the world by living according to his or her state of life and with a deep concern for the needs of all
- brings the message of the Good News by a faith-filled, love-filled life and willingly shares gifts and talents for the good of the kingdom of God
- possesses an open, loving spirit toward all persons of all religions who strive to live a spiritual life
- attempts to bring peace to all by working for justice and love in all life's situations

Documents of Vatican II

The Constitution on the Sacred Liturgy
Liturgy as the focus of community worship and piety; liturgical renewal and more active participation of laity.

Book One
508*766*771*824*971

Book Two
1067*1068*1070-1072*1074-1076*1086*1088-1090*1100*
1113*1123*1140*1141*1143*1144*1156-1158*1163*1166*
1167*1172-1176*1181*1183*1193*1194*1203-1205*1232*
1255*1298*1323*1346*1373*1388*1398*1438*1482*1513*
1514*1517*1548*1552*1561*1570*1621*1667*1669*1670*
1675*1684*1685

Book Three
2132*2191*2503*2513

Decree on the Means of Social Communication
Responsibility and challenges of the media. Use of the media to promote faith and values.

Book Three
2494*2495*2498

Dogmatic Constitution on the Church

Church as people of God; permanent diaconate restored.

Book One

87*90*92*93*165*337*375*488-490*492-494*499*501*506*
507*511*541-543*562*567*669-671*748*753-757*759*
761-764*766-769*771*773*775*776*781*782*784-786*788*
790*791*793*798*801*804*810*811*814-816*819*823-829*
831-833*835-839*841*843*844*846*847*853*860-862*
870-872*874*880-889*891-898*900*901*904*905*908*
909*912-915*917*932*933*938*943*951*954-960*
963-972*1001*1013*1023*1036*1042*1045*1050

Book Two

1076*1090*1093*1119*1120*1141*1202*1249*1251*1257*
1260*1269*1270*1273*1281*1285*1303*1312*1324*1364*1373*
1405*1422*1426*1428*1440*1444*1462*1469*1499*1522*1535*
1538*1546-1549*1551*1552*1554-1562*1564*1566*1567*
1569-1571*1575*1576*1582*1588*1620*1621*1641*1656*1657

Book Three

1816*1888*1986*2003*2013*2028*2032*2034*2035*
2045*2068*2103*2132*2204*2225*2226*2545

Book Four

2674*2679

Decree on the Catholic Eastern Churches

Addressed to Uniate Churches of Eastern rites; recognizes diversity in rites and encourages retaining traditions.

Book Two

1389

Decree on Ecumenism

Encourages Christian unity; respects others beliefs; sets forth guidelines for interfaith endeavors.

Book One
90*94*812*813*815-822*824*827*838*855*925

Book Two
1126*1202*1271*1399*1400

Book Four
2791

Decree on the Pastoral Office of Bishops in the Church

Collegiality of bishops as sharing authority with the pope; calls for Synods of Bishops.

Book One
833*882*886*927*937

Book Two
1548*1558*1560*1569*1586

Decree on the Up-to-Date Renewal of Religious Life

Call to renewal of relevance and challenge to religious to live in conformity to gospel values.

Book One
915*916*918*929

Book Two
1620

Book Four
2684*2691

Decree on the Training of Priests

Priestly training and continuing formation; calls for evaluation of seminary curricula.

Book Two
1565*1620

Declaration on Christian Education

Value of education to values; parents have prime responsibility for moral training of their children.

Book Two
1653

Book Three
2221*2229

Declaration on the Relation of the Church to Non-Christian Religions

Sees sacredness in non-Christian religions as valid approaches to the Divine; respects Judaism especially as the root of Christianity; anti-Semitism condemned.

Book One
360*597*839*841-843

Book Three
2104

Book Four
2793

Dogmatic Constitution on Divine Revelation
Scripture and Tradition as main sources of Revelation; primacy of the Word of God in both Old and New Testaments.

Book One
36*38*51*53-55*62*64*66*74-82*84-86*94*95*97*98*101*
103-107*109-111*119-122*124-126*129*131 133*135*136*
141-143*153*158*337*573*889*891

Book Two
1094*1103*1124*1346

Book Three
1814

Book Four
2587*2650*2651*2653*2663

Decree on Apostolate of Lay People
Holiness is call for everyone. Laity involvement in the Church; bringing the gospel into the world.

Book One
798*851*863*864*873*905*940

Book Two
1570

Book Three
2044*2105*2446

Book Four
2832

Declaration on Religious Liberty

Conscience as the basic norm of morality; dignity and rights of the human person; condemnation of all types of discrimination.

Book One
160

Book Two
1180

Book Three
1738*1782*1785*1816*2036*2104-2109*2137*2467

Decree on the Church's Missionary Activity

All share in the missionary work of the Church; evangelization is more effective by example than by direct tactics.

Book One
248*257*294*763*767*776*804*830*848-850*
852-854*856*857*868*877*905*927

Book Two
1233*1248*1249*1257*1260*1270*1344*1560*1570*1571

Book Three
2472

Decree on the Ministry and Life of Priests
Priests are called to integrate their lives with work and spirituality; pastoral dimension of the priestly life.

Book One
888

Book Two
1102*1122*1141*1142*1175*1181*1324*1369*1392*1464*1466*
1548*1562*1563*1565*1566*1568*1579*1580*1582

Book Four
2686

Pastoral Constitution on the Church in the Modern World
Church and world as mutually related; dignity of all persons; marriage and family, culture, society, economics, politics, and peace issues.

Book One
27*29*33*49*94*159*308*339*356*358*359*364*367*372*
382*383*390*401*409*415*421*450*470*520*521*618*676*
776*813*853*854*942*1006*1008*1018*1048-1050

Book Two
1251*1260*1535*1603*1612*1627*1632*1639*1642*1645*1646*1652*
1657*1660*1664

Book Three

1701*1703-1707*1710-1713*1730*1743*1776*1791*1794*
1795*1878*1879*1881*1882*1892*1901*1902*1906-1908*
1911*1912*1915-1917*1920*1924*1931*1935*1936*1938*
1955*1958*2123-2126*2184*2194*2206*2210*2227*2242*
2245*2246*2250*2268*2271*2304*2306-2308*2310-2312*
2314*2317*2322*2329*2334*2339*2344*2362*2364*2367*
2368*2371*2373*2387*2404*2406*2408*2419*2420*2424*
2426*2427*2434*2527

Book Four

2783*2799*2820

Other helpful resources from Liguori Publications

Faith for the Future
A New Illustrated Catechism
A Redemptorist Pastoral Publication

This book is what all catechisms should be…reader friendly. It is 200 pages of compelling catechetical reading that is both informative and entertaining. With one look, catechists will see its appeal. Full color throughout, with incredible attention paid to graphic detail, it is fully indexed to the *Catechism*. Scriptural references and quotes, historical anecdotes, and doctirne make *Faith for the Future* great for Catholic information. **$12.95**

What You Should Know About
the Catechism of the Catholic Church
Charlene Altemose, MSC

Thoroughly explains the new *Catechism*. Provides a useful historical background to the *Catechism,* explains its rationale and purpose, and addresses the individual's response in faith to the *Catechism*. Also discusses practical use of the *Catechism* in classroom study, personal study, Adult Initiation, group discussion, and more. **$1.95**

Handbook for Today's Catholic Family
A Redemptorist Pastoral Publication

Offers a great depth of understanding, hope, and help for today's Catholic families. Suggests family activities and prayers to help foster family closeness and Catholic identity. **$4.95**

Liguorian magazine

Almost 1 million Catholics enjoy this leading Catholic magazine. Each month it offers information, inspiration, and motivation. There's something for everyone with features for children and teens, articles for singles, married couples, and seniors. **$20.00 per year** *(includes postage and handling).* Outside U.S.A., please add $7.00.

Order from your local bookstore or write
Liguori Publications
Box 060, Liguori, MO 63057-9999
Please add 15% to your total for postage and handling ($3.50 minimum, $15 maximum). For faster service call toll-free 1-800-325-9521, Dept. 060. Please have your credit card handy.